MECHANIC MACHINE TOOL MAINTENANCE FIRST YEAR MCQ

OBJECTIVE QUESTION ANSWERS

MANOJ DOLE

Digitization is the need of the time. In the future, training in industrial training institutes will need to be conducted using online internet to make training more convenient and easy. E-books containing a set of MCQ questions will be made available to the trainees as they need to be more accustomed to the multiple choice questions MCQ to prepare for the online exams taking place in their industrial training institutes.

With all these factors in mind, Mr. Manoj Madhukar Dole Instructor, Industrial Training Institute, Satara, has written books according to the new annual system and NSQF-5 syllabus. And they've created theoretical mobile apps and blogs to make training easier, and made all these educational materials available for download on the world famous websites Google Play Store, Amazon and Apple Book Store.

The books were published by Hon'ble Joint Director Shri Rajendra Ghume Saheb Regional Office of Vocational Education and Training, Pune on 9/1/2019, at this time Shri Prakash Saigavkar Saheb Principal Government Industrial Training Institute Aundh Pune, Shri Tukaram Misal Saheb Principal Govt. Q. Sanstha Satara, Shri Sachin Dhumal Saheb District Vocational Education and Training Officer Satara, Shri Yatin Pargaonkar Saheb Principal Govt. Q. Sanstha Kolhapur, Shri Vikas Teke Saheb Inspector Vocational Education and Training Regional Office Pune, Palekar Foods Products Pvt. Ltd. Entrepreneurial Chairman of Satara Mr. Nilkanthrao Palekar Saheb, Chairman of Hira Foods Mr. Ibrahim Baba Tamboli Saheb, Mrs. Shalmali Pawar Headmaster Government Technical School Center Satara and other dignitaries were present on the occasion.

Contents

Prologue

Mechanic Machine Tool Maintenance A is a simple e-Book for ITI Engineering Course Mechanic Machine Tool Maintenance (MMTM) , First Year, Sem- 1 & 2, Revised NSQ F-5 Syllabus in 2022, It contains objective questions with underlined & bold correct answers MCQ covering all topics including all about safety aspect related to trade, basic fitting operation viz., marking, filling, sawing, chiseling, drilling tapping & grinding, different fits viz., sliding, T-fit & square fit, shaping and milling operation, power transmission elements, operation of lathe machine and making of different components, machine foundation and geometrical tests, preventive maintenance of machines viz., lathe, drilling, milling, and lots more.

We add new question answers with each new version. Please email us in case of any errors/omissions. This is arguably the largest and best e-Book for All engineering multiple choice questions and answers.

As a student you can use it for your exam prep. This e-Book is also useful for professors to refresh material.

Foreword

Vocational education and training is imparted through the Department of Vocational Education and Training through the Department of Business Education and Business Practical to supply multi-skilled artisans in line with the rapidly growing demand in the industrial sector in the 21st century. All the occupations within the institutions are important, as the trainees from these occupations develop multi-skills as per the demands of the industry.

with the noble intention of making available MCQ e-books suitable for all businesses, considering that all the examinations in all the industries in the industrial sector are conducted online and include MCQ method questions. Mr. Manoj Madhukar Dole has written a very good e-book on MCQ method as per the new annual syllabus. This e-book will definitely be a guide for all the trainees, trainee candidates, training instructors and others concerned.

The author of the book is Mr. Manoj Madhukar Dole, Instructor Gov. ITI Satara has 17 years of training experience. Written as a new annual pattern, this e-book incorporates modern digital QR Code technology to understand the layout, simple language, and simple syntax, diagrams and videos for each subject. So I am sure that this e-book will definitely be useful for in-depth study and exam practice. The work they have done is certainly commendable.

Mr. Tukaram Misal
Principal Government Industrial Training Institute Satara.

Preface

DGET New Delhi and CSTARI Kolkata have been implementing an annual pattern for all businesses in ITI since the August 2018 session. The examination system will also be changed and it will be online from this year and since all the questions are of Objective Type (MCQ), the trainees are in dire need of in-depth study. It is with this in mind that we are delighted to present the books based on the old NIMI pattern and a complete overview of the new annual pattern, and we hope that these books will be a guide for all business directors and trainees. Is.

For writing these books, Johar Awate Saheb, Principal of ITI Akluj. Former Principal of ITI Satara Saigavkar Saheb, Assistant Director Shri Chandrakant Dhekne Saheb Regional Office of Vocational Education and Training, Pune, District Vocational Education and Training Officer Sachin Dhumal Saheb and Headmaster Government Technical School Kendra Shalmali Pawar Madam and son Adhiraj Dole, mother Kusum Dole, I am very grateful to my father Madhukar Dole and wife Ashwini Dole for their special guidance and cooperation from time to time.

Also, in a very short period of time, the book was reviewed by Shri Rajendra Ghume Saheb, Joint Director, Vocational Education and Training Regional Office, Pune, for his invaluable time in publishing the book. I am sincerely grateful for their feedback.

I am grateful to the Instructor of ITI Satara for there continuous support from the very beginning of writing the book.

From this book, I consider myself blessed to have shared my thoughts on e-learning with you. I will not claim that this book is perfect, because considering the perfection, this book is an attempt and is in its infancy. They will be valuable for improvement if they are tested and suggested.

Manoj Dole
Dated 9/1/2019

Acknowledgements

The industrial training and theoretical examination system of our industrial training institutes and these changes have been accepted by the craft instructors and the trainees. Theoretical examinations conducted in your industrial training institutes are also conducted online. Since these examinations are of multiple choice MCQ method, the trainees will need to get more practice of such questions.

With all these considerations in mind, Mr. Manoj Madhukar, Director, Dole Crafts, Katari Industrial Training Institute, Satara, has done a thorough study and with his diligent work and added his keen intellect, according to the new annual system and NSQF-5 syllabus, e-book of Katari and other machine trades. -Book) and they have created mobile apps and blogs on theoretical topics to make training easier and have made all these educational materials available for download on the world famous websites Google Play Store, Amazon and Apple Book Store. Training has been made easier by creating a print version and using advanced techniques like QR Code.

All these educational materials will definitely be a guide for all the trainees for in-depth study and for the craft instructors and other concerned who are imparting vocational training.

CHAPTER ONE

Mechanic Machine Tool Maintenance First Year MCQ Drawings

www.itibook.blogspot.com www.itiapp.blogspot.com www.ititests.blogspot.com

www.itibook.com

Fire extinguisher

Calliper

www.itibook.blogspot.com www.itiapp.blogspot.com www.ititests.blogspot.com

www.itibook.com

Hacksaw frame

Universal surface guage

Hammer

Centre punch

Bench vice

Files

Scraper

Surface Plate

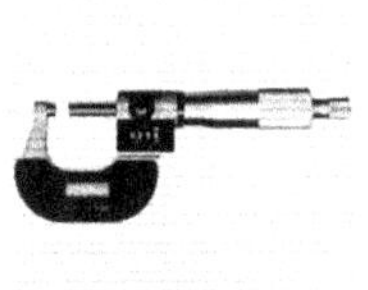

Outside Micrometer

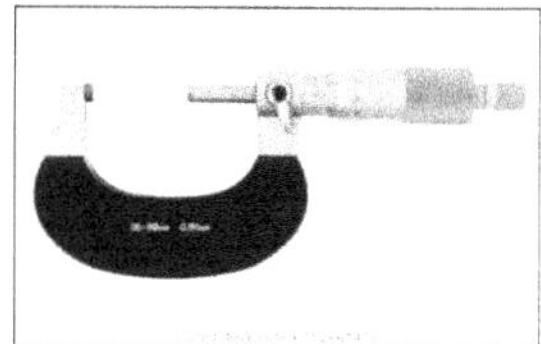

Micrometer

Depth micrometer

Vernier Calliper

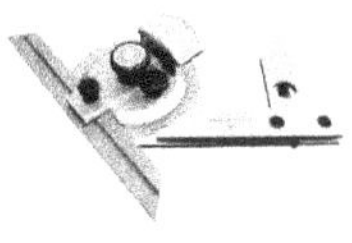

www.itibook.blogspot.com www.itiapp.blogspot.com www.ititests.blogspot.com

www.itibook.com

Vernier bevel protractor

Drilling

Reamer

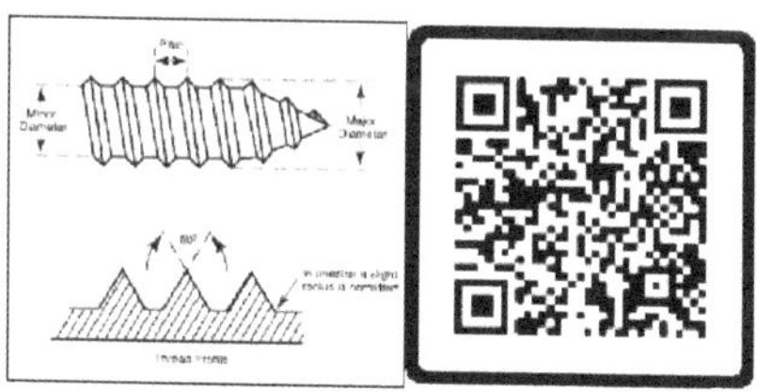

Thread

Tap Die

Grinding Wheel

Slip gauge

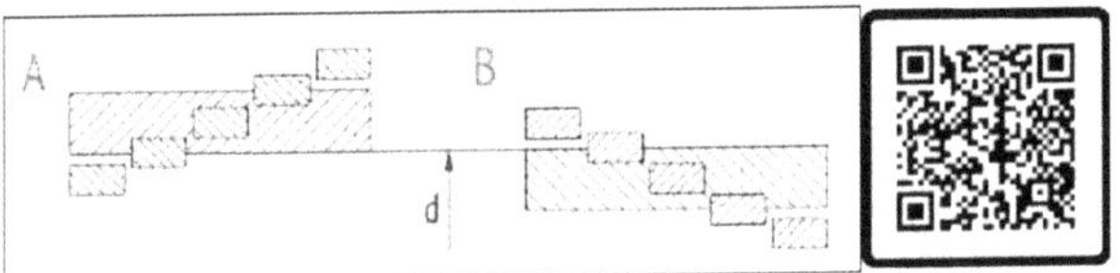

Limit fit tolerance

Lathe Machine

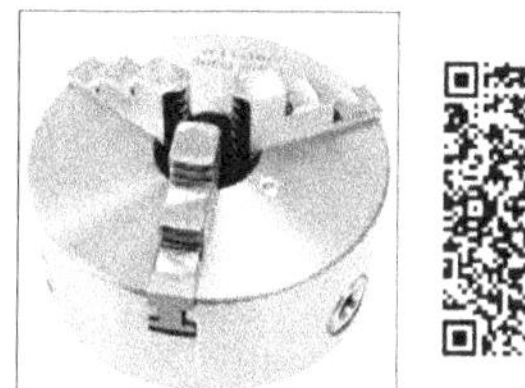

Lathe chuck

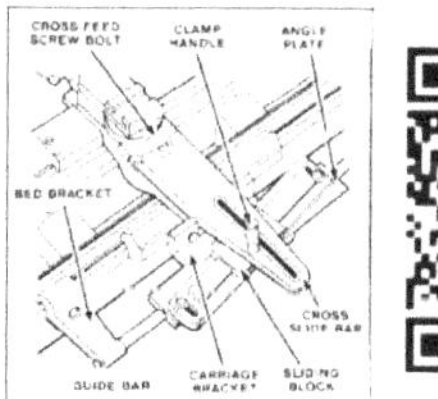

Taper turning attachment

taper ring gauge

screw pitch gauge

Gear

screw pitch gauge

Tap Die

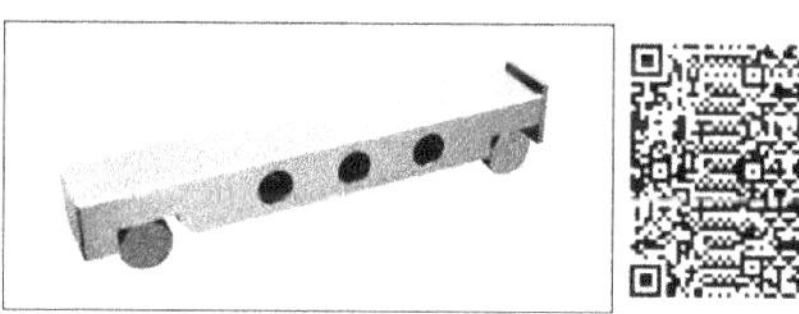

Sine bar

www.itibook.blogspot.com www.itiapp.blogspot.com www.ititests.blogspot.com

www.itibook.com

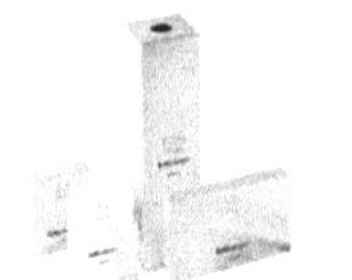

Slip gauge

Dial test indicator

Telescopic gauge

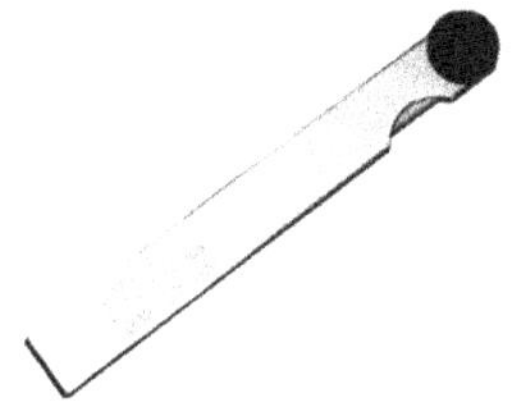

Feeler gauge

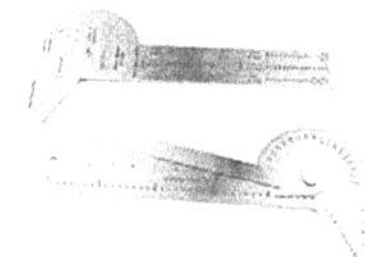

Centre gauge

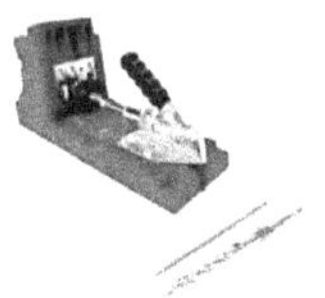

Jig

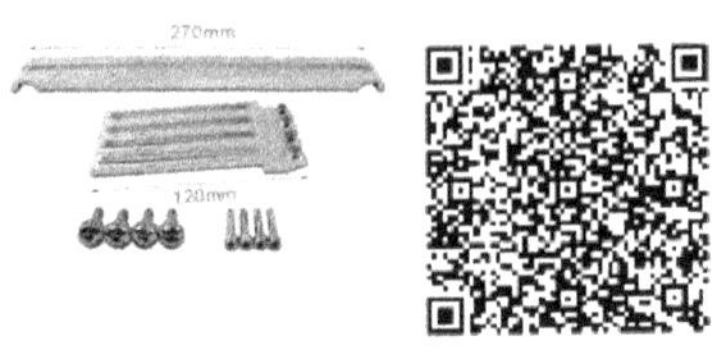

Fixture

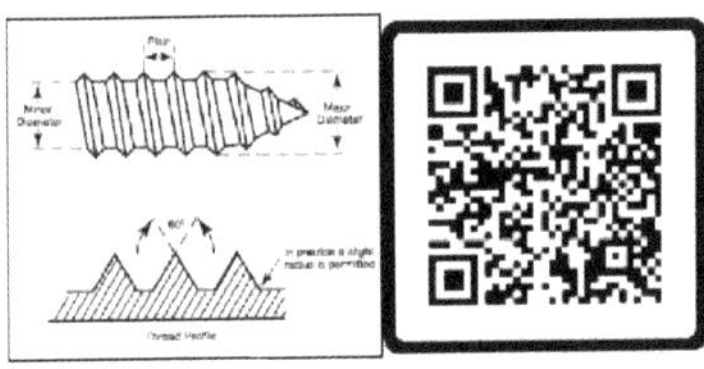

Thread

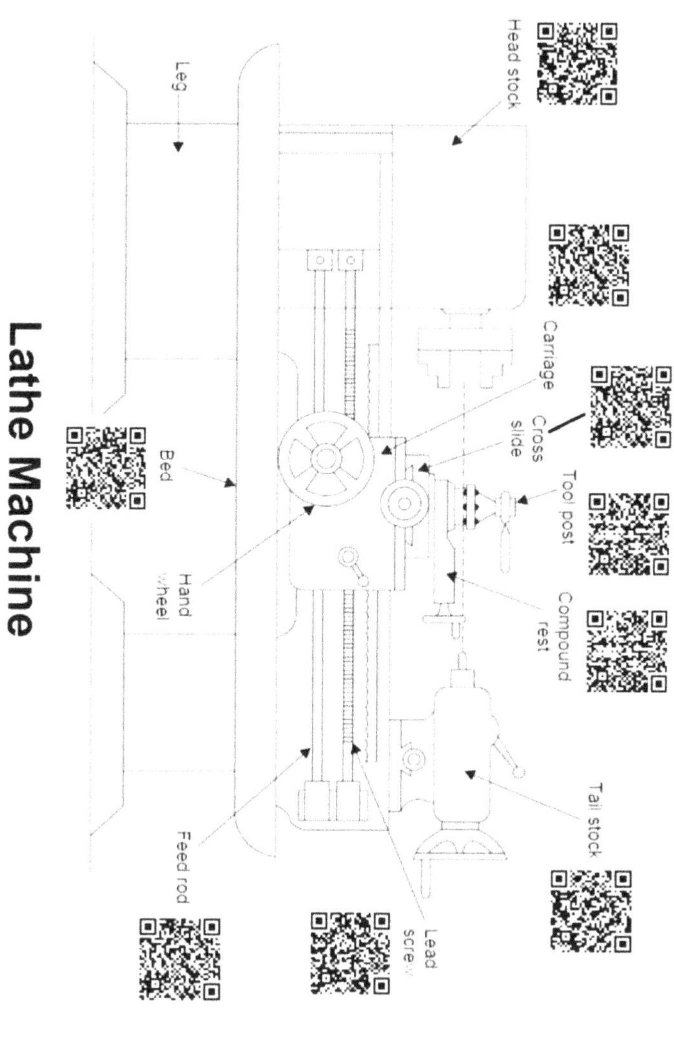
Lathe Machine
Head stock
Leg
Carriage
Cross slide
Tool post
Bed
Hand wheel
Compound rest
Tail stock
Feed rod
Lead screw

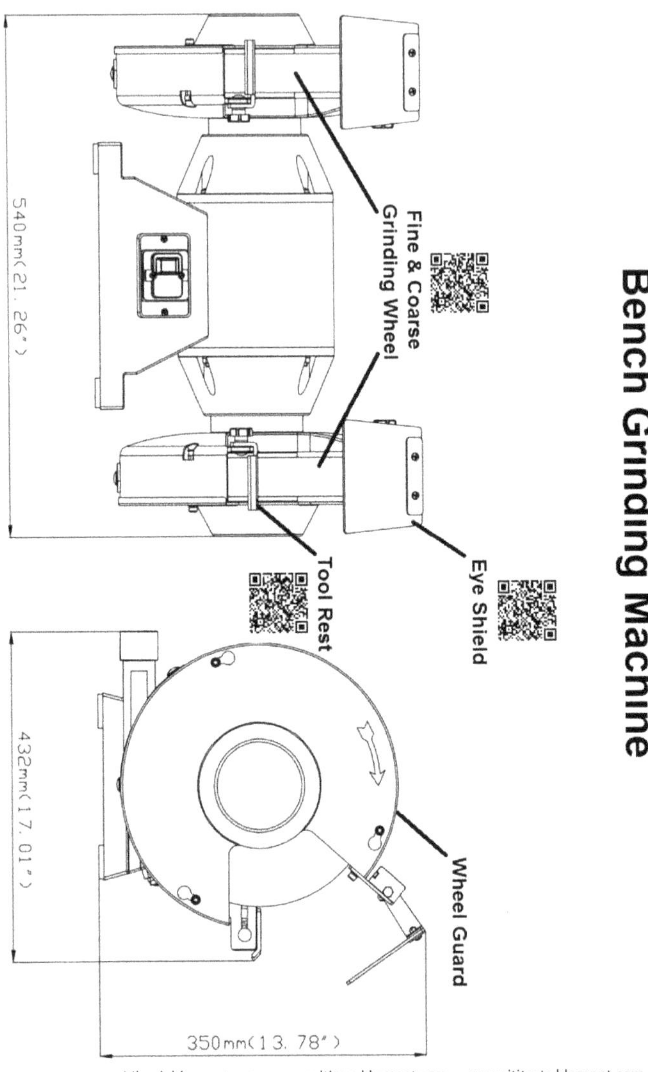

www.itibook.blogspot.com www.itiapp.blogspot.com www.ititests.blogspot.com

www.itibook.com

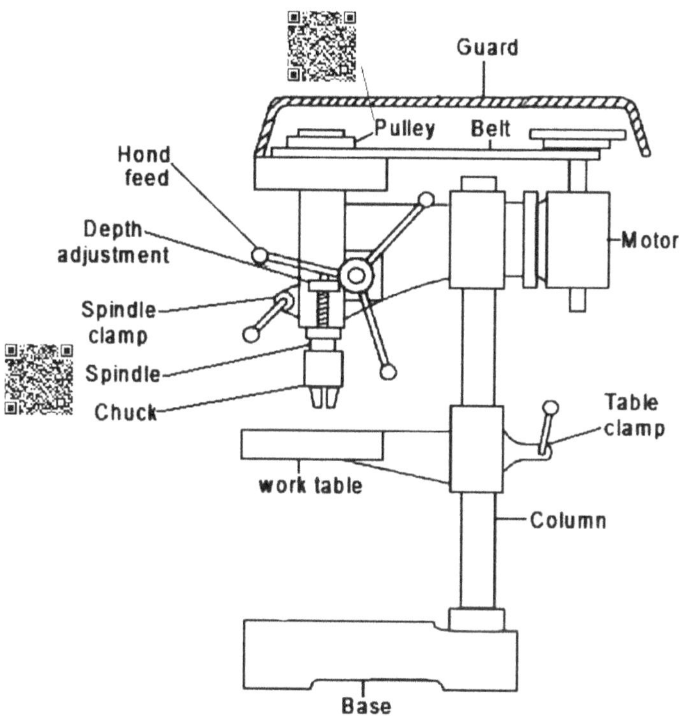

Piller Drilling Machine

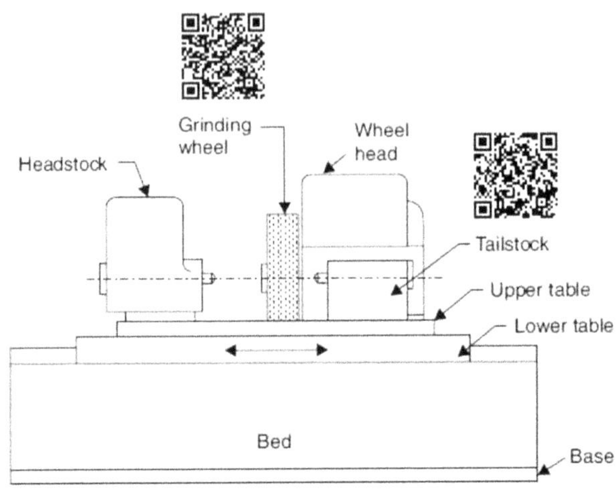

plain cylindrical grinder

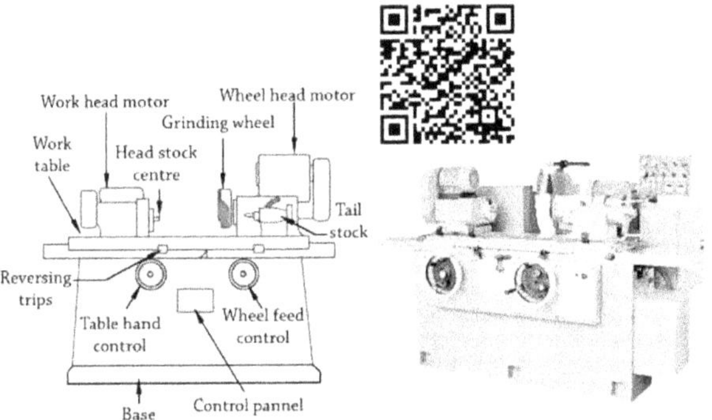

Cylindrical grinding machine

To study Different operations and parts of Surface Grinding Machine

SURFACE GRINDER

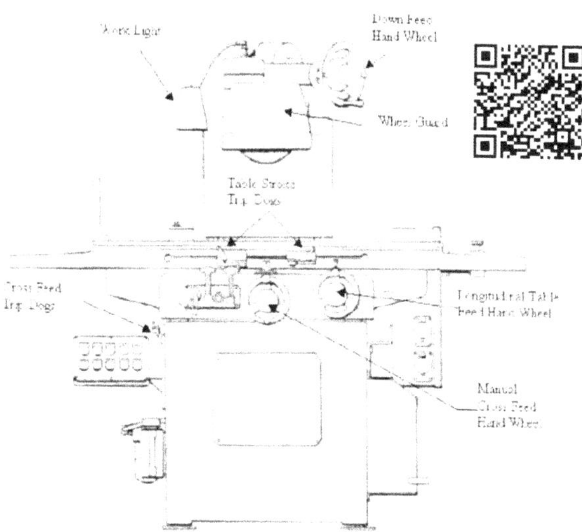

Surface grinding is used to produce a smooth finish on flat surfaces. It is a widely used abrasive machining process in which a spinning wheel covered in rough particles (grinding wheel) cuts

PLAIN OR HORIZONTAL MILLING MACHINE

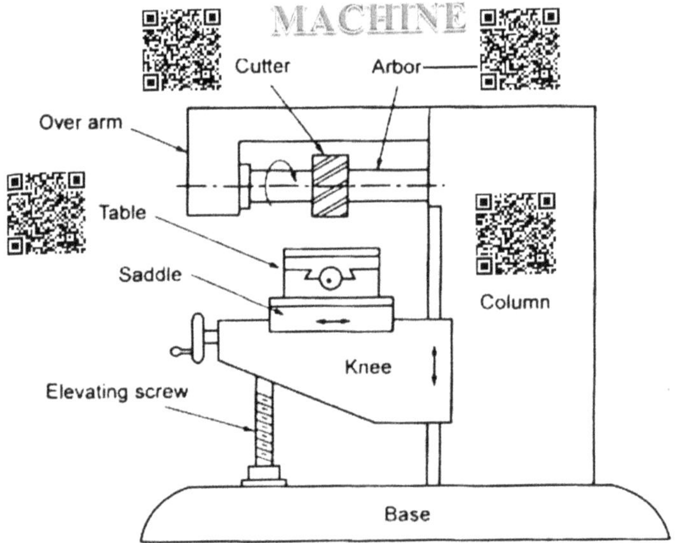

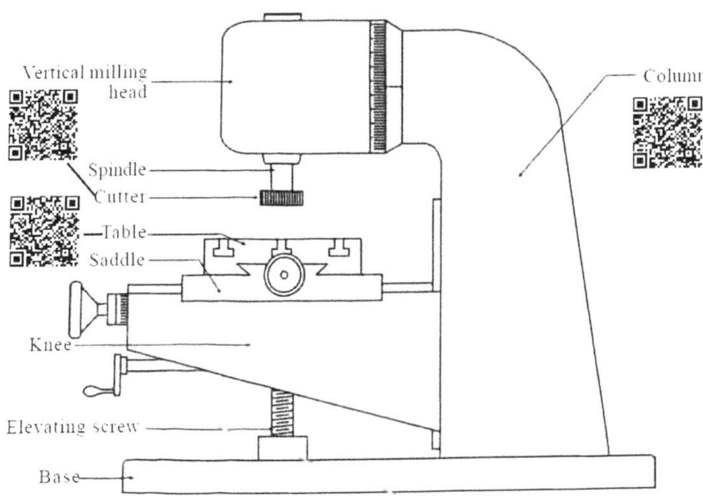

Vertical Milling Machine

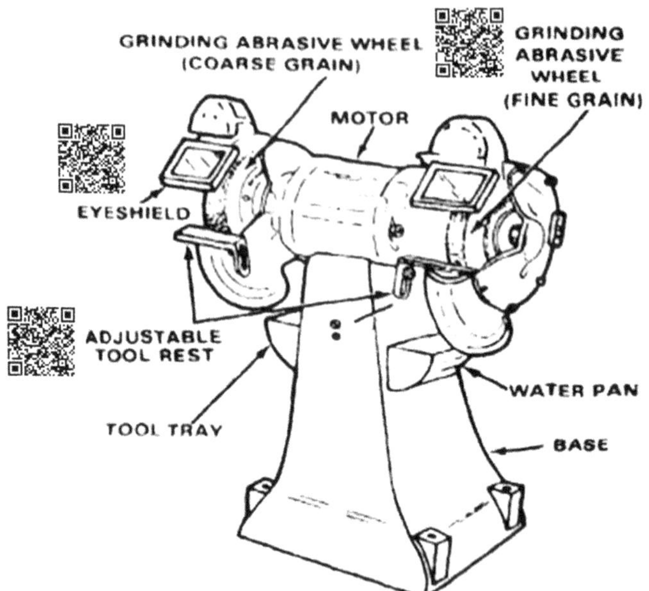

Pedastal Grinding Machine

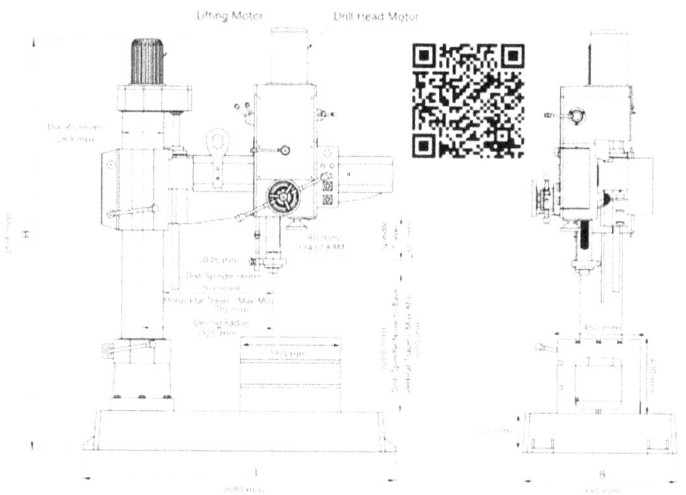

Radial Drilling Machine

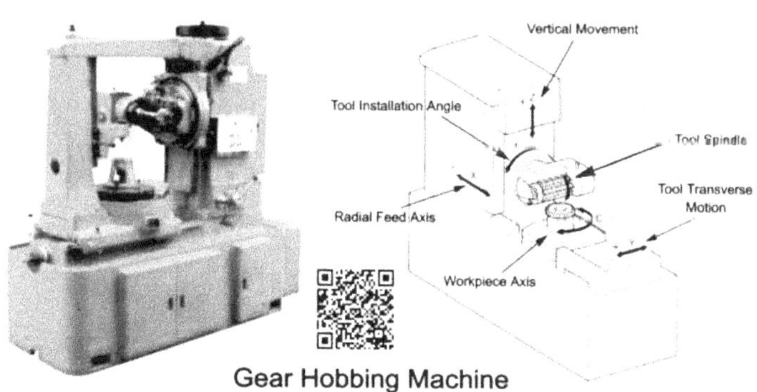

Gear Hobbing Machine

DOUBLE HOUSING PLANER

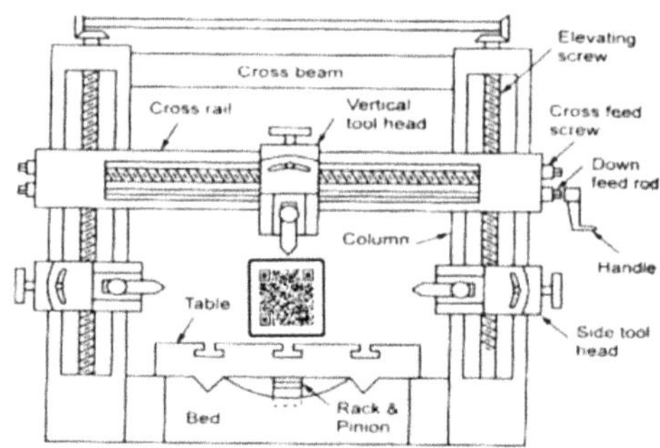

PIT PLANER

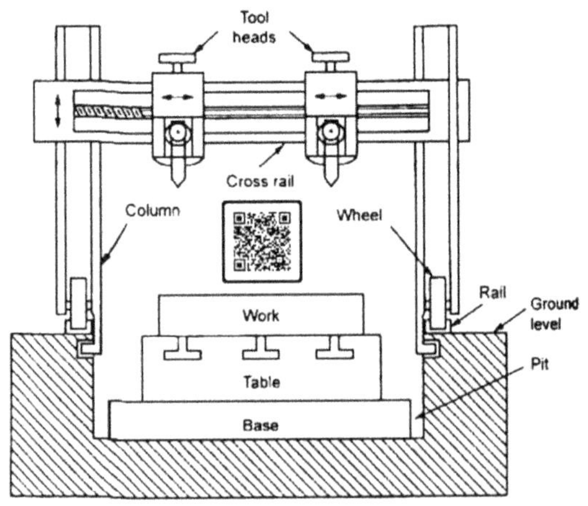

OPEN SIDE PLANER

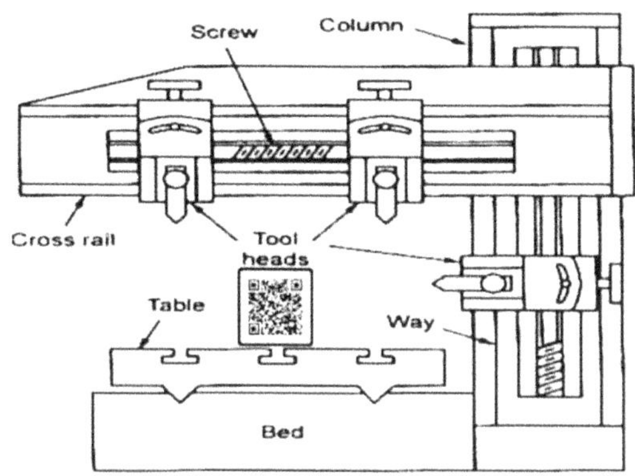

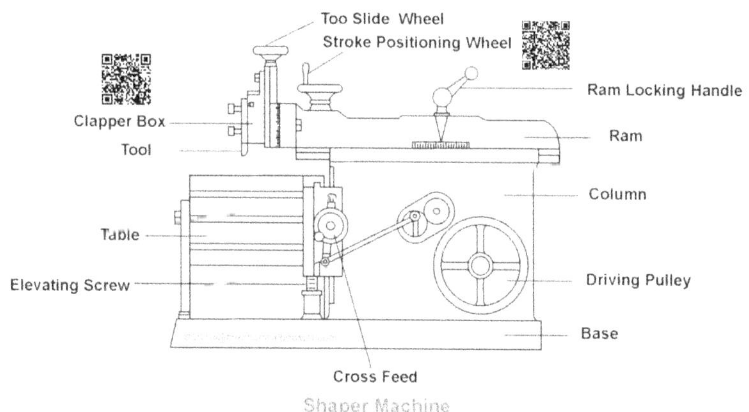

Shaper Machine

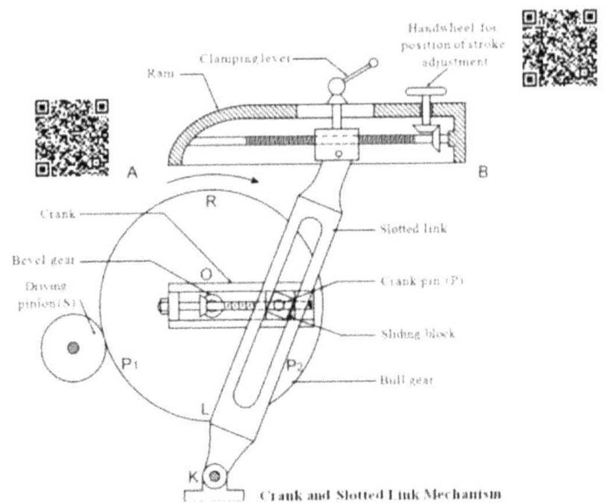

Quick Return Mechanism of Shaper Machine

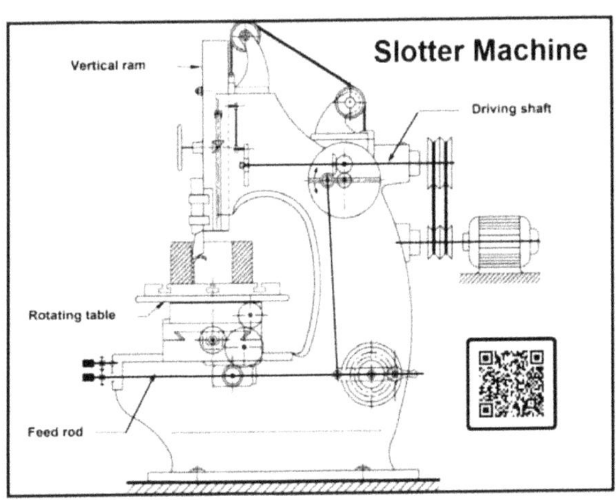

CHAPTER TWO

Mechanic Machine Tool Maintenance First Year MCQ

01] In case of bleeding, take treatment Of

D] cold 3" and rest

<u>A] spray cold water</u>

B] Bandage immediately -----

B] Enquire about the accident thought treatment

02] in case of an accident, the victim should im

A] Asked to take rest

<u>C] Attended immediately</u>

D] leave him

03] First aid is given to an injured or ill person primarily

A] Save life

B] Prevent further deterioration of the muff's

C] Give best possible comfort

<u>D] All of these</u>

04] Colour code for Bins for waste paper segregation is -----

<u>A] blue Colour</u>

B] Yellow Colour

C] Red Colour

D] Green Colour

05] In Japanese Seiko stands for -------------

<u>A] Shine</u>

B] Sort

C] Standardize

D] Sustain

06] Benefit of SS system is ------

A] Increase in productivity

B] Increase in quality

C] Reduction in wastage of time

D] All of these

07] Safety is -----------

A] nobody's business

B] every bodise business

C] Some bodies business

D] The organization business

08] For basic categories of safety signs are available The meaning of"prohibition" sign ----

A] shows it must not be done

B] Shows what must be done

C] Warns the hazard or danger

D] Gives information of safety provision

09] Which one is a workshop safety?

A] Keep shop floor clean and free from grease, oil or other slippery materials

B] Stop the machine before changing the speed

C] Don't use cracked or chipped tools

D] Don't try to stop a running machine with hand

10] In Personal Protect Equipment (PPE] HELMET is used to

A] protect head

B] Protect eyes

C] Protect hands

D] Protect ears

11] Which of the following belongs to general safety?

A Have a worker in good attitude

B] The work clean and clear

C] Concentrate on your work

D] Keep the floor and gangways clean and clear

12] While grinding, which is used to protect the eyes?

A] Dark green glass

B] Mask

C] Sun glasses

D] Safety goggles

13] Which of the following is done for machine safety?

A] Check the oil level before starting the machine

B] Do things in a methodical way

C] Keep the floor and gangways clean and clear

D] Don't use dies and scarves

14] In Personal Protect Equipment (PPE], 'sleeves' is used to protect ----------

A] Face

B] Eyes

C] Ears

D] Hands

15] ABC stands for --------------

A] Automatic Breathing Control

B] Automatic Blood Control

C] Airway Breathing Circulation

D] Automatic Blood Circulation

16] To put off"Class B" fire, the types of fire extinguisher used is

A] dry power

B] Carbon dioxide

C] Jet of water

D] Foam type

fire extinguisher Animation Videos

17] Which type of fire extinguisher is used to put off general fire?

A] Water type Extinguisher

B] Foam type Extinguisher

C] Dry chemical powder Extinguisher

D] Carbon dioxide (C02] Extinguisher

18] One micrometer (U] is equal to

A] 01mm

B] 001mm

C] 0001mm

D] 00001mm

19] The caliper meant for measuring the width of a slot is

A] Odd leg caliper

B] Outside caliper

C] Jenny caliper

D] Inside calliper

Callipers Animation Videos

20] The size of the dividers are specified by the ----------

A] Total length of legs

B] Distance between the points when fully opened

C] Length of legs without points

D] distance between the pivot and the point

21] The instrument used to mark parallel lines, parallel to the datum edge is -

A] jenny caliper

B] Divider

C] Outside calliper

D] Inside calliper

22] Which one of the following is an indirect measuring tool?

A] Outside caliper

B] Vernier calliper

C] Steel rule

D] Outside micrometer

23] For cutting thin tubing, the most suitable pitch of the hacksaw blade is

A] 18mm

B] 14mm

C] 1mm

D] 08mm

24] For cutting solid brass, the most suitable pitch of the hacksaw blade is

A] 18mm

B] 14mm

C] 1mm

D] 08mm

25] A new hacksaw blade after a few strokes becomes loose because of the

A] Stretching of the blade

B] Wing-nut threads being worn out

C] Wrong pitch of the blade

D] Improper selection of the set of saws

Hacksaw frame Animation Videos

26] While cutting small diameter pipes, it is advisable to watch regularly and ensure that

A] The cut is along the curved line

B] More saw teeth are in contract

C] The work is not overheated

D] Proper balancing of hacksaw is maintained

27] The vice clamps are used to

A] Protect hard jaws

B] Clamp the work pieces rigidly

C] Protect the finished surfaces

D] Prevent the movable jaw being filed

28] The reference surface during marking is provided by the

A] Surface gauge

B] Workpiece

C] Drawing of the work

D] Marking table surface

29] The size of an engineer's vice is specified by the

A] Length of the movable jaw

B] Width of the jaws

C] Height of the vice

D] Maximum opening of the jaws

30] The part of the universal surface gauge which helps to draw a parallel line along a datum edge is the

A] Rocker arm

B] Snug

C] Fine adjustment screw

D] Guide pins

31] Scribers are made of

A] Mild steel

B] High carbon steel

C] Brass

D] Cast iron

32] Portion of the hammer used for fixing the handle is

A] Face

B] Peen

C] Cheek

D] Eye hole

Hammer Animation Videos

33] Weight of the hammer for the marking purpose is

A] 250g

B] 500g

C] 1 kg
D] 2 kgs
34] The size of the dividers are specified by the
A] Total length of the legs
B] Distance between the points when fully opened
C] Length of legs without the points
D] Distance between the pivot and the point
35] The included angle of the groove of 'V' block is always
A] 45◦
B] 60◦
C] 90◦
D] 120◦
36] 'V' blocks are available in grades of
A] A & B
B] A,B & C
C] 1,2 & 3
D] 1 & 2
37] 'V' blocks of grade 'B' are made of
A] Cast iron
B] Mild steel
C] Steel
D] Cast steel
38] Ribs are given on the unmachined portion of the angle plate for
A] Easy handling
B] Convenience in manufacturing
C] Clamping while setting on machines
D] Rigidity and to prevent distortion
39] The slots on the angle plate are given for
A] Reducing weight
B] Aligning the work
C] Lifting using hooks
D] Accommodating bolts
40] The size of the angle plates is stated by
A] Weight
B] Length
C] Length x width
41] Name the punch used to locate the centre
A] Prick punch 30°

B] Prick punch 60°

C] Centre punch

D] Dot punch

centre punch Animation Videos

42] The point angle of centre punch is --------

A] 30°

B] 50°

c] 900

D] 1200

43] Punches are used for forming ---------of any shape

A] Holes

B] Mining

C] Knurling

D] Reaming

44] Generally the length of the handle of the vice is ----------

A] 15 times the normal size of the vice

B] 25 times the normal size of the vice

C] 35 times the normal size of the vice

D] 45 times the normal size of the vice

Bench vice Animation Videos

45] Bench vice spindle is made of

A] mild steel

B] Cast iron

C] Tool steel

D] Bronze

46] The convexity of files helps

A] To file concave surfaces

B] To file convex surfaces

C] To prevent rounding of edges of work

D] The file to become straight when pressure is applied

Files Animation Videos

47] Which file used for filling wood, leather and other soft material?

A] Single cut file

B] Double cut file

c] Rasp cut file

D] Curved cut file

48] File used is used for ------------

A] Cleaning the work piece
C] Renewing the file teeth
B] cleaning the file teeth
D] Cleaning the chips
49] File card is used to --------
A] Clean the work piece
C] Renew the file teeth
B] Clean the file teeth
50] The point angle of scriber is -----------
A] 30°
B] 60°
C] 5° to 10°
D] 12° to 15°
51] The cutting angle for chipping cast iron is
A] 375◦
B] 55◦
C] 60◦
D] 90◦
52] The chisel will dig into the material when
A] The rake angle is more
B] The clearance angle is too low
C] The angle of inclination is more
D] The angle of inclination is too low
53] A slight convexity is given to the cutting edge to
A] Cut curved surfaces
B] Cut sharp corners
C] Prevent digging of the ends
D] Allow the lubricant to enter
54] Surface plates are made of
A] High grade cast steel
B] Fine-grained cast iron
C] Alloy steels
D] Wrought iron
55] The taper shank drills are held on the machine by means of
A] Chucks
B] Sleeves
C] Drift
D] Vice

56] Drill chucks are fitted on the drilling machine spindle by means of a

A] Knurled ring

B] Arbor

C] Drift

D] Pinion and key

57] The Morse taper provided on drills ranges between

A] MT 1 to MT 5

B] MT 1 to MT 4

C] MT 0 to MT 5

D] MT 0 to MT 4

58] A drift is used for

A] Drawing a drill location

B] Fixing chuck on the machine spindle

C] Removing a broken drill from the work

D] Removing the drill from the machine spindle

59] When the taper shank of the drill is larger than the machine spindle, the device to hold the drill is a

A] Drill sleeve

B] Taper socket

C] Drill drift

D] Chuck and key

60] The suitable cutting fluid for drilling mild steel in a drilling machine is

A] Synthetic soluble oil

B] Neat oil

C] Distilled water

D] Soluble oil

61] A special feature of the radial drilling machine is

A] It can be used for drilling with a HSS drill

B] Table can be moved and set at any position

C] A variety of speeds is available

D] The spindle can be brought to any position

62] The point angle of drills depends on

A] The size of the drill

B] The type of machine

C] The material of the work

D] The RPM of the drill

63] The point angle for a standard drill is

A] 60°

B] 108°

C] 118°

D] 135°

64] The helical angle determines the

A] Cutting angle

B] Chew angle

C] Rake angle

D] Lip angle

65] The clearance angle of the drill is between

A] 3° to 5°

B] 8° to 12°

C] 12° to 20°

D] 15° to 20°

66] In a remote place (no electricity available] a rail track is to be drilled Choose the right drilling machine

A] Radial drilling machine

B] Pillar drilling machine

C] Ratchet drilling machine

D] Sensitive drilling Machine

Drilling Animation Videos

67] A drilling machine used by a carpenter for cabinet making is a

A] Ratchet drilling machine

B] Radial drilling machine

C] Breast drilling machine

D] Sensitive drilling machine

68] Which one of the following drilling machines is used for drilling holes where electricity is not available?

A] Bench drilling machine

B] Pillar drilling machine

C] Redial drilling machine

D] Ratchet drilling machine

69] Which one of the following drilling machine is used for heavy duty work?

A] Bench drilling machine

B] Pillar drilling machine

C] Radial drilling machine

D] Electric hand drilling machine

70] Drill chuck are held on the machine spindle by means of ------

A] arbor

B] Drift

C] draw-in bar

D] Chuck nut

71] Different speeds are obtained in a sensitive bench drilling machine by ----

A] Belt pulley mechanism

B] Hydraulic mechanism

C] Rack and Pinion mechanism

D] Cam and follower mechanism

72] Tap are re sharpened by grinding -----

A] Hutes

B] Threads

C] Diameter

D] Relief

73] The tapping drill size for M10 x 15 is ----------

A] 82

B] 83

C] 84

D] 85

74] A nut is to be made for a screw of M10XIS What should be the size of drilled hole?

A] 8-5 mm

B] 90 mm

C] 95 mm

D] 100 mm

75] A die in which more than one cutting operation is per formed in one stroke

A] Piercing die

B] Progressive die

C] Combination die

D] Compound die

Tap Die Animation Videos

76] A die in which cutting and non cutting operations are carried out per stroke

A] Piercing die

B] Progressive die

C] Combination die

D] Compound die

77] A die in which two or more sequential operations are performed at two or more stations upon the work

A] Piercing die

B] Progressive die

C] Combination die

D] Compound die

78] A die in which the shape of the punch and die are directly reproduced in the metal with little or no metal flow

A] Progressive die

B] Combination die

C] Compound die

D] Forming die

79] The die used for producing any shape of holes

A] Piercing die

B] Progressive die

C] Combination die

D] Compound die

80] A short reamer with an axial hole used with an arbor or mandrel is called -------

A] Parallel reamer

B] Adjustable reamer

C] Expansion reamer

D] Chucking reamer

Reamer Animation Videos

81] Which one of the following machine reamers is used to correct the misalignment between the reamer axis and the work axis?

A] Floating blade reamer

B] Machine jig reamer

C] Shell reamer

D] Chucking reamer

Jig

82] Accuracy or least count of a metric outside micrometer is ---------

A] 0-1 mm

B] 001 mm

C] 0001 mm

D] 002 mm

83] 1000 microns means -----

A] 1 mm

B] 1 m

C] 1000 mm

D] 10 cm

84] in a metric micrometer, a complete revolution of thimble advances -----------

A] 001 mm

B] 025 mm

C] 050 mm

D] 100mm

Micrometer Animation Videos

85] Ratchet Stop in the micrometer helps to ------------

A] Control the pressure

B] lock the spindle

C] Adjust the zero error

D] Hold the work piece

86] 1000 micron means ------------

A] 1 mm

B] 1 m

C] 1000 mm

D] 10 cm

87] What is the zero reading of a 50-75 mm outside micrometer?

A] 0000 mm

B] 001 mm

C] 2500 mm

D] 5000 mm

88] The value of the smallest division on sleeve of a metric outside micrometer is -----

A] 050 mm

B] 100 mm

C] 150 mm

D] 200 mm

89] Ratchet stop in the micrometer helps to ---------

A] control the pressure

B] Lock the spindle

C] Adjust the zero error

D] Hold the work piece

90] Least count of depth micrometer is

A] 0.5 mm

B] 0.2 mm

C] 0.001 mm

D] 0.01 mm

91] in which one of the following micrometer the graduations on thimble and sleeve are in reverse direction to that of outside micrometer?

A] Inside micrometer

B] Depth micrometer

C] Tube micrometer

D] Flange micrometer

Depth micrometer Animation Videos

92] The graduations of a depth micrometer is ----------

A] in the reverse direction to that of the outside micrometer both thimble and sleeves

B] In the reverse direction only of the sleeve

C] In the reverse direction only on the thimble

D] Similar to an outside micrometer

93] The pitch of the spindle of a depth micrometer is --------in metric pitch.

A] 0.01 mm

B] 0.02 mm

C] 0.3 mm

D] 0.5 mm

94] The least count of vernier calliper is (main scale = 49 division, vernier scale = 50 division]

A] 0.1 mm

B] 0.01 mm

C] 0.001 mm

D] 0.02 mm

Vernier Calliper Animation Videos

95] The type of measurement made by using a Vernier Calliper is -------

A] Direct measurement

B] Indirect measurement

C] 90“] (a] 81 (b]

D] None of these

96] The least count of a vernier bevel protractor is

A] 1”

B] 5’

C] 1◦

D] 5 ◦

97] The part of a vernier bevel protractor which is normally used as a reference base for measuring angles is the

A] Blade

B] Stock

C] Disc

C] Main scale

Vernier bevel protractor Animation Videos

98] The part of a vernier bevel protector on which main scale divisions are marked is the

A] Stock

B] Dial

C] Disc

D] Adjustable blade

99] The part of a bevel protractor, which comes in contact with the inclined surface while measuring is the

A] Blade

B] Stock

C] Disc

D] Dial

100] The value of each division of the main scale of a vernier bevel protractor is

A] 5'

B] 1°

C] 5°

D]10°

101] The value of each division of the vernier scale of a bevel protractor is

A] 1°

B] 1°5'

C] 1°55'

D] 5'

102] The function of the Pedestal grinder includes -----

A] Sharpening of the cutting tool

B] Rough grinding

C] Both (a] & (b]

D] None of these

103] The type of abrasives used for the two wheels of Pedestal Grinder are-

A] Coarse and Coarse type

B] Fine and fine type

C] Coarse and fine

D] None of these

104] The Operation of shaping of the grinding wheel by dressers?

A] Dressing

B] Truing

C] Clogging

D] glazing

Grinding Animation Videos

105] Dressing and truing of the grinding wheel are --------

A] Exactly the same operation

B] Clone with the same equment

C] Done only for coarse grinding wheel

D] Only for form grinding

106] The process of enlarging the end of a hole for accommodating the socket screw head is

A] Reaming

B] Spot facing

C] Counter boring

107] Appropriate tool used for spot facing operation is

A] Reamer

B] Counter sinks

C] Fly cutters

108] The cutting speed for aluminium with HSS tools is

A] 30 m/min

B] 50 m/min

C] 70 m/min

D] 130 m/min

109] The cutting speed for brass with a HSS tool is

A] 10 m/min

B] 25 m/min

C] 70 m/min

D] 140 m/min

110] The distance, which the cutting edge of a tool passes over the material in a minute while machining is Know as

A] RPM

B] Feed

C] Machine speed

D] Cutting speed

111] By using coolants on work pieces we can choose

A] Higher cutting speeds

B] lower cutting feeds

C] lower cutting speeds

D] heavy depth of cuts

112] Suitable for low cutting speed and feed rates

A] Carbon steel cutters

B] Sintered carbide tool cutters

C] Ceramics cutters

D] Diamond cutters

Miling cutters Animation Videos

113] Extremely high cutting speed with low feed rate for precision finishing]

A] Carbon steel cutters

B] Sintered carbide tool cutters

C] Ceramics cutters

D] Diamond cutters

114] By using coolants on work pieces we can choose

A] higher cutting speeds

B] lower cutting feeds

C] lower cutting speeds

D] heavy depth of cuts

115] When using a diamond wheel for cutter grinding, a wheel speed of 1600/mm is recommended] What should be the depth of cut?

A] 0005-0025mm

B] 0025-004mm

C] 004-005mm

D] 005-005mm

116] The depth of cut for M24 x 3 mm internal thread is

A] 05412 x 3

B] 06134 x 3

C] 05 x 3

D] 07 x 3

Thread Animation Videos

117] The depth of cut for metric square threading is

A] 06 x P

B] 05 x P

C] 05412 x P

D] 06412 x P

118] To cut buttress thread, the depth of cut is

A] 05412 x P

B] 06 x P

C] 07 x P

D] 075 x P

119] Tennon slots are provided on arbor shoulder

A] To facilitate insertion of key between cutter and arbor at any position
‘

B] To facilitate positive power transmission to the arbor

C] To ’ facilitate interchangeability of arbors and machines

D] To avoid loosening of arbor nut during cutting action]

120] In the BIS system of limits and fits, the grade of tolerance are represented by number Symbols and there are ---------i

A] 14 grades of tolerance

B] 16 grades of tolerance

C] 18 grades of tolerance ‘

D] 20 grades of tolerance

Limit fit tolerance Animation Videos

121] A Product is said to have the quality when

A] Its shape and dimensions are within the limit

B] It is fit for use

C] It appears to be very good

D] The choice of material is right

122] The maximum clearance required between hole'30 +0021, 0000 and shaft 30 -0110, 0143 is

A] 0110 mm '

B]0131 mm

C] 0164 mm

D] 0143 mm

123] A dimension is stated as 25 1002 mm in a drawing What is the tolerance?

A] +002 mm'

B] +004 mm

C] -002 mm

D] 2500 mm

124] A pin is fitted in a hole The tolerance zone of the pin is entirely above that of hole The fit obtained will be?

A] Clearance fit

B] Transition fit

C] Interference fit

D] Running fit

125] Tolerance is given to the part size to

A] Production the part within the required permissible size error

B] Increase the production

C] Decrease the Production

D] Finish the components approximately

126] Which one of the following is the clearance fit under the whole basic system?

A] 20 H7/p6'

B] 2067/211

C] ZOG/gll

D] 20H/g11

127] The three classes of fits as per BIS system aré

A] Clearance fit, interference fit and transition fit

B] Medium fit, push fit and tight fit

C] Flat fit, round fit and square fit

D] 'Sliding fit ', loose fit and shrinkage fit

128] Which one of the following tolerance specifications has a maximum dimensionless than 20 mm?

A] 20 +02,-03

B] 20 3202

C] 20 -02, 03 e

D]m 20 +500, ~03

129] Difference between the maximum and minimum limit is --------------------

A] Single informant

B] Basic shaft

C] Clearance

D] Tolerance

130] A shaft 55 running freely in bush bearing the type of fit is ---------

A] Clearance fit

B] Driving plate

C] shrinkage fit

D] None of the above

131] helps to tool to lifts up during return stroke

A] clapper box of shaper

B] rocker arm

C] pawl and ratchet

D] bull gear

132] pivoted at the bottom of the base

A] clapper box of shaper

B] rocker arm

C] pawl and ratchet

D] bull gear

133] meant for feed mechanism

A] clapper box of shaper

B] rocker arm

C] pawl and ratchet

D] bull gear

134] helps to tool to lifts up during return stroke

A] clapper box of shaper

B] rocker arm

C] pawl and ratchet

D] bull gear

135] driven by pinion

A] clapper box of shaper

B] rocker arm

C] pawl and ratchet

D] bull gear

136] it carries the saddle
B] rocker arm
C] pawl and ratchet
D] bull gear
E] cross rail
137] it is mounted on bull gear face
A] clapper box of shaper
B] rocker arm
C] pawl and ratchet
D] bull gear
138] it slips during return stroke.
A] clapper box of shaper
B] rocker arm
C] pawl and ratchet
D] bull gear
139] Can be swivelled while shaping angular surfaces
B] Clapper block
C] Tool post
D] Hinged pen
E] Swivel base
140] it is a device for holding the cutting tool and for setting the depth and position of a cut
A] Clapper box
B] Clapper block
C] Tool post
D] Hinged pen
141] During return stroke the clapper box is free to swivel about it.
A] Clapper box
B] Clapper block
C] Tool post
D] Hinged pen
142] Holds the tool or tool holder rigidly
A] Clapper box
B] Clapper block
C] Tool post
D] Hinged pen
143] Lifts during of return stroke
A] Clapper box

B] Clapper block

C] Tool post

D] Hinged pen

144] The movement of the vertical slide in achieved by stating this part.

D] Hinged pen

E] Swivel base

F] Vertical slide

G] <u>Feed screw handle</u>

145] Bench grinder are used for

A] Heavy duty work

B] Heavy and light duty work

<u>C] Light duty work</u>

D] Lather work

146] Bench Grinders are fitted on a

A] Base

<u>B] Table]</u>

C] Wheel guards

D] Conveyor

147] Which one of the following is the most commonly used Precision grinding machines?

A] Surface grinders

B] Tool cutter grinders

C] Cylindrical grinders

<u>D] All of these</u>

148] The feeler gauge is used for...

A] Checking surface roughness

B] Checking the redius of workpieces

C] <u>Checking the gap between mating parts</u>

D] Checking the accuracy of the hole locators

Feeler gauge Animation Videos

149] Generally gauges are made out of

A] nickel chromium

B] mild steel

C] cast steel

D] H.S.S.

150] Generally gauges are used for

A] mass production

B] measuring the components

C] individual component

D] checking the dimensional accuracy

151] Spindle is perpendicular to the work table

A] Horizontal milling machine

B] Vertical milling machine

C] Universal milling machine]

D] Lathe machine

152] The table can be swivelled in horizontal plane

A] Horizontal milling machine
B] Vertical milling machine
C] Universal milling machine]
D] Lathe machine
153] The spindle is horizontal to the work table
A] Horizontal milling machine
B] Vertical milling machine
C] Universal milling machine]
D] Lathe machine
154] Rigid, sturdy and accommodates heavy work
A] Horizontal milling machine
B] Vertical milling machine
C] Universal milling machine]
D] Lathe machine
155] Boring, keyway cutting, profile milling can be done on this machine
A] Horizontal milling machine
B] Vertical milling machine
C] Universal milling machine]
D] Lathe machine
156] Helical grooves and gears can be milled on this machine
A] Horizontal milling machine
B] Vertical milling machine
C] Universal milling machine]
D] Lathe machine
157] Slide movement on the column
A] Longitudinal feed
B] Cross feed
C] Vertical feed
D] Circular feed]
158] Slide movements on the knee
A] Longitudinal feed
B] Cross feed
C] Vertical feed
D] Circular feed]
159] Rotary table
A] Longitudinal feed
B] Cross feed
C] Vertical feed

D] Circular feed]

160] Table traverse]

A] Longitudinal feed

B] Cross feed

C] Vertical feed

D] Circular feed]

161] produces surface perpendicular to the axis of cutter

A] is face milling process

B] is side milling process

C] is plain milling process

D] is end milling process

162] producing surfaces vertical and flat, perpendicular to the machine arbor

A] is face milling process

B] is side milling process

C] is plain milling process

D] is end milling process

163] cutting is done at end and periphery to make slots

A] is face milling process

B] is side milling process

C] is plain milling process

D] is end milling process

164] The process done on plain milling machine

A] is face milling process

B] is side milling process

C] is plain milling process

D] is end milling process

165] The process done on vertical milling machine

A] is face milling process

B] is side milling process

C] is plain milling process

D] is end milling process

166] Composition of cobalt tungsten carbide and tentalum carbide

A] Carbon steel cutters

B] Sintered carbide tool cutters

C] Ceramics cutters

D] Diamond cutters

167] A composition of oxides of aluminium and silicon or magnesium

A] Carbon steel cutters

B] Sintered carbide tool cutters

C] Ceramics cutters

D] Diamond cutters

168] Steel with11%to 15% carbon

A] Carbon steel cutters

B] Sintered carbide tool cutters

C] Ceramics cutters

D] Diamond cutters

169] Suitable for low cutting speed and feed rates

A] Carbon steel cutters

B] Sintered carbide tool cutters

C] Ceramics cutters

D] Diamond cutters

170] Extremely high cutting speed with low feed rate for precision finishing]

A] Carbon steel cutters

B] Sintered carbide tool cutters

C] Ceramics cutters

D] Diamond cutters

171] More brittle in nature

A] Carbon steel cutters

B] Sintered carbide tool cutters

C] Ceramics cutters

D] Diamond cutters

172] is used to cut flutes on reamers

A] Equal double angle cutter

B] Bore type single angle cutter

C] Unequal double angle cutters

D] shank type single angle cutter]

173] is used to cut dovetail guide ways on a horizontal milling machine

A] Equal double angle cutter

B] Bore type single angle cutter

C] Unequal double angle cutters

D] shank type single angle cutter]

174] is used to cut 'V' grooves

A] Equal double angle cutter

B] Bore type single angle cutter

C] Unequal double angle cutters

D] shank type single angle cutter]

175] has two types as type 'A', type 'B' based on the diameter of the small end

A] Equal double angle cutter

B] Bore type single angle cutter

C] Unequal double angle cutters

D] shank type single angle cutter]

176] is Specified by mentioning two angles

A] Equal double angle cutter

B] Bore type single angle cutter

C] Unequal double angle cutters

D] shank type single angle cutter]

177] may or may not have cutting edges at flat side]

A] Equal double angle cutter

B] Bore type single angle cutter

C] Unequal double angle cutters

D] shank type single angle cutter]

178] Vertical milling attachment

A] face milling, boring, end drilling, 'T' slot milling

B] milling longer milling racks

C] mounted on the face of the column or the over arm

D] vertical milling attachment is provided

179] For using plain or universal milling machine as a vertical milling machine

A] face milling, boring, end drilling, 'T' slot milling

B] milling longer milling racks

C] mounted on the face of the column or the over arm

D] Vertical milling attachment is provided

180] Vertical attachments enable the horizontal milling machine to perform

A] face milling, boring, end drilling, 'T' slot milling

B] milling longer milling racks

C] mounted on the face of the column or the over arm

D] vertical milling attachment is provided

Milling attachment Animation Videos

181] The rack milling attachment and rack indexing attachment used for

A] face milling, boring, end drilling, 'T' slot milling

B] milling longer milling racks

C] mounted on the face of the column or the over arm

D] vertical milling attachment is provided

Indexing head Animation Videos

182] Slotting attachment converts the rotary motion of spindle

A] vertical milling attachment is provided

B] can be turned through 90x in either direction

C] to increase the versatility' of the machine

D] into reciprocating motion

183] Milling attachments are designed]

A] vertical milling attachment is provided

B] can be turned through 90x in either direction

C] to increase the versatility' of the machine

D] into reciprocating motion

184] attachment is useful involving light machining

A] Gear cutting attachment

B] Spherical turning attachment

C] Relieving attachment]

D] None of above

Gear Animation Videos

185] tool advancement is] controlled by the cam profile

A] Gear cutting attachment

B] Spherical turning attachment

C] Relieving attachment]

D] None of above

186] usefulforcutting splines etc

A] Gear cutting attachment

B] Spherical turning attachment

C] Relieving attachment]

D] None of above

187] Which one of the following is the resistance of a metal to elastic deformation?

A] Ductility

B] Strength

C] Stiffness

D] Toughness

188] The process of heating and cooling to change the structure of steel for obtaining the required properties is called

A] Hardening

B] Normalizing

C] Heat treatment

D] Tempering

189] The main purpose of annealing is to

A] Increase the hardness

B] Increase the toughness

C] Improve machinability

D] Improve distortion

190] The purpose of normalizing steel is to ----------

A] Remove the induced Stress

B] Improve genes and reduce brittleness

C] Soften the metal

D] Increase the surface?

191] Which one of the following process is used for hardenmg the outer 5" Annealing

A] Hardening

B] Tempering

C] Case Hardening

D] Tear surface

192] The purpose of producmg a component with tough and ductIle core and hard ou is known as

A] Hardening

B] Case hardening

C] Tempering

D] annealing

193] Lower critical temperature of high carbon steel while hardening is ----------

A] 9600C

B] 900°C

c] 7230 c

D] 56O C

194] The process of Changing the structure and thus changing the properties by heating and 'cooling is known as --

A] Heat treatment

B] Alloying

C] Tempering

D] None of these

195] For refining the grain structure which one of the following heat treatment processes 'Is adopted

A] Annealing

B] Hardening

C] Tempering

D] Normalising

196] Annealing is performed on iron and steel ---------

A] To remove internal stresses

B] To reduce hardness

C] To improve machinability

D] All of these

197] Which one of the following does not fall under the stages of heat treatment?

A] Heating

B] Cleaning

C] Quenching

D] Soaking

198] Gun metal is an alloy of copper, ------------

A] tin and zinc

B] Lead and zinc

C] Zinc and nickel

D] Lead and nickel

199] for making gutters, roof flashing, hoods etc

A] Galvanised iron

B] Stainless steel

C] Copper sheet

D] Metal sheets

200] in dairies food processing, kitchen ware etc

A] Galvanised iron

B] Stainless steel

C] Copper sheet

D] Metal sheets

201] for making buckets, heating ducts, cabinets etc

A] Galvanised iron

B] Stainless steel

C] Copper sheet

D] Metal sheets

202] in canneries and chemical plants Metal sheets

A] Galvanised iron

B] Stainless steel

C] Copper sheet

D] Metal sheets

203] Alloy steel, good corrosive resistance and welds easily

A] Black iron
B] Galvanised iron
C] Stainless steel
D] Aluminium

204] Cheapest, can be rolled to any desired thickness
A] Black iron
B] Galvanised iron
C] Stainless steel
D] Aluminium

205] Resists against rust bright silvery appearance
A] Black iron
B] Galvanised iron
C] Stainless steel
D] Aluminium

206] Corrodes rapidly Bluish black appearance
A] Black iron
B] Galvanised iron
C] Stainless steel
D] Aluminium

207] Used for scraping large flat surfaces
A] Bull-nose scraper
B] Three-square
C] Half round scraper
D] None of above

208] Used for scraping small scraper diameter holes and for deburring of holes
A] Bull-nose scraper
B] Three-square
C] Half round scraper
D] None of above

209] Used for scraping bearing surfaces which are neither too big nor too small
A] Bull-nose scraper
B]Three-square
C] Half round scraper
D] None of above

210] Used for scraping large diameter holes
A] Bull-nose scraper

B] Three-square
C] Half round scraper
D] None of above
211] Used where bolt and threads are to be protected from damage.
A] Donald cap nut
B] Thumb nut
C] Hexagonal nut
D] Wing-nut
212] Used where frequent removal and fixing is required.
A] Donald cap nut
B] Thumb nut
C] Hexagonal nut
D] Wing-nut
213] Used in machine building and structure work.
A] Donald cap nut
B] Thumb nut
C] Hexagonal nut
D] Wing-nut
214] Used where frequent adjustments are to be made.
A] Donald cap nut
B] Thumb nut
C] Hexagonal nut
D] Wing-nut
215] Nylon inserts in the nut prevent loosening.
A] Locking plate
B] Wire lock
C] Self-locking nut
D] Sawn nut
216] A slot is cut halfway across the nut.
A] Locking plate
B] Wire lock
C] Self-locking nut
D] Sawn nut
217] Prevents slackening of two bolts.
A] Locking plate
B] Wire lock
C] Self-locking nut
D] Sawn nut

218] Prevents rotation of the top nut.

A] Lock-nut

B] Grooved nut

C] Self-locking nut

D] Sawn nut

219] Prevents loosening of nut by the use of a plate shaped to fit the nut.

A] Locking plate

B] Wire lock

C] Self-locking nut

D] Sawn nut

220] Hexagonal nut with the lower part made cylindrical and the recessed groove.

A] Lock-nut

B] Grooved nut

C] Self-locking nut

D] Sawn nut

221] Drill a blind hole equal to half of the diameter of the stud. Insert this tool into the hole and remove the stud by turning this anticlockwise.

A] Prick Punch Method

B] Filing square very mm

C] Using square taper punch

D] Ezy-out method

222] If the stud is broken near to the surface, employ this method to remove the stud.

A] Prick Punch Method

B] Filing square very mm

C] Using square taper punch

D] Ezy-out method

223] When a stud is broken a little above the surface this method is used to remove the stud.

A] Filing square very mm

B] Using square taper punch

C] Ezy-out method

D] Making drill hole

224] To extract the broken stud a special tool is employed in this method.

A] Prick Punch Method

B] Filing square very mm

C] Using square taper punch

D] Ezy-out method

225] Used on finished tubular surfaces to avoid marking

A] Stillson pipe wrench

B] Chain wrench

C] Strap wrench

D] Foot print wrench

226] Used for gripping and turning pipes and round stocks in confined pieces

A] Stillson pipe wrench

B] Chain wrench

C] Strap wrench

D] Foot print wrench

227] Used for holding large diameter pipes

A] Stillson pipe wrench

B] Chain wrench

C] Strap wrench

D] Foot print wrench

228] Used for gripping and turning pipes, tubes and cylindrical rods]

A] Stillson pipe wrench

B] Chain wrench

C] Strap wrench

D] Foot print wrench

229] Rivets for Joining sheets to thick plates.

A] Countersunk head

B] Flat head

C] Pan head

D] Mushroom

230] Rivets for Joining sheet metal.

A] Countersunk head

B] Flat head

C] Pan head

D] Mushroom

231] Rivets for Heavy fabrication work.

A] Countersunk head

B] Flat head

C] Pan head

D] Mushroom

232] Rivets for Reduces the height of rivet head above the meta\ surface
A] Countersunk head
B] Flat head
C] Pan head
D] Mushroom
233] Rivets for commonly used for structural work.
A] Countersunk head
B] Flat head
C] Pan head
D] Snap head
234] Grinding with a balanced grinding wheel will make it p05
A] dimensional accuracy with surface finish
B] Pattern Of lapsable to achieve the required ----
C] Position tolerance surface finish only
D] Positional tolerance
235] The purpose of finish milling is to ....
A] Bring the work piece to required dimension and surface finish
B] Bring the work piece to required dimension
C] Bring to the required surface dimension
D] Remove less material.
236] ln case of ant burr on slip gauge, it should be removed by
A] Filling
B] Lapping
C] Scraping
D] Grinding
237] The stops and trips are used to
A] minimise delays for measuring and gauging
B] minimise delays in setting tools
C] reduce the number of tools needed
D] reduce the time required to set work]
238] The tern surface finish refers to the...
A] Shining of a machined surface
B] Type of coating given on a surface
C] Heat treatment given on a surface
D] Roughness or smoothness of a surface
239] The purpose for which lapping operation are carried out ---
A] To refine surface finish]
B] To improve quality of fit

C] To improve geometrical accuracy,

D] All the above

240] Which one of the following is a cold working process by which improvement of surface finish, dimensional accuracy and work hardening can be affected without removal of metal?

A] Burnishing

B] Honing

C] Lapping _

D] Super finishing

241] In the honing Process, the movement of the spindle is ---‘ -----------

A] Vertical and reciprocating

B] Reciprocating

C] Vertical

D] Horizontal and reciprocating

242] It is the process carried out by using abrasive stick?

A] Lapping

B] Honing

C] Super finishing ‘

D] Burnishing

243] Which one of the following is important factor required to achieve the interchange ability in mass production?]

A] Geometrical accuracy]

B] Standardization

C] Dimensional accuracy

D] Surface finish

244] Sine bar is made of

A] high carbon steel

B] high speed steel

C] nickel steel

D] stabilized chromium steel]

Sine bar Animation Videos

245] Sine bar is used for

A] levelling the job for drilling

B] finding the angle of taper job

C] measuring diameter of holes

D] checking profile of thread]

246] Length of sine bar is the distance between

A] one end to another end of sine bar

B] diagonal cross length of the sine bar

C] centre to centre between rollers

D] outside to outside between rollers]

247] The size of a sine bar is specified by it's

A] weight

B] measurement of width

C] length

D] maximum angle of setting]

248] The purpose of providing a stopper at one end of the sine bar is for

A] easy handling

B] preventing the job from slipping]

C] supporting the slip gauge

D] using as a reference while setting]

249] A sine bar is made with four or five equally'spaced holes on its body] The purpose of these holes is to

A] Handle the sine bar easily

B] Reduce the weight of sin bar

C] Prevent distortion of the top surface of sine bar

D] Give good appearance to the sine bar

250] A sine bar is used for

A] Measuring the diameter of holes '

B] Finding the angle of a taper job

C] Leveling the job for drilling

D] Chuckin'g the profile of a thread

251] For measuring angles using the sine bar the angle framed according to the ratio between the height of slip gauge and the

A] Height of sine bar

B] Number slip gauge

C] Length of sine bar

D] Width of sine bar

Slip guage Animation Videos

252] -----------is used for checking angle within an accuracy of 1

A] Gauge

B] Sine bar

C] Temple

D] Telescopic gauge

253] Centre line of the contact rollers and datum surface if the sine bar are

A] Same line' '

B] Parallel

C] Inclined

D] Perpendicular

254] The sine bar is made of .

A] High carbon steel

B] Stabilized chromium steel '

C] High speed steel

D] Nicked steel

255] A sine bar with a length of l=200mm is used to check accurately the angle of a Work piece] The angle to be checked: 250 calculate the height 'h' of the slip gauges?

A] 84.54mm

B] 83.52mm

C] 81.81mm

D] 85.52mm

256] Which of the following statement is correct?'

A] Gauges are used to check the size

B] Template are used to chuck-the size

C] Gauges are used to measure the size

D] Gauges are used to check shape of component

257] At what standard temperature are the gauges kept in the section?

A] 100 C

B] 20° C

C] 100 F

D] 20° F

258] Which grade of slip gauge is generally used in workshop?

A] Grade 0

B] Grade l

C] Grade H

D] Grade 0

259] As per Indian Standards a special set gauge is used consisting of

A] 81 Pieces

B] 112 Pieces

C] 120 Pieces

D] 130 Pieces

260] The accuracy of reference gauge is

A] 0.05 mm

B] 0.01 mm

C] 0.001]

D] 0.0001 mm

261] ln case of ant burr on slip gauge, it should be removed by

A] Filling

B] Lapping

C] Scraping

D] Grinding

262] Hardness of slip gauge should be?

A] More than 63 HRC

B] 58 HRC

C] 55 HRC

D] 50 HRC

263]------------- Slip gauge is used for Checking component within an accuracy of 0.01 mm]

A] Workshop gauge

B] Inspection gauge

C] Reference gauge

D] Ring gauge

264] ------------is used for checking accuracy of precision instrument]

A] Gauge block

B] Fader gauge

C] Sine bar

D] Plug gauge

265] Slip gauge are Cleaned before using to ensure accuracy] What medium will you use for this purpose.

A] Oil

B] Thinner

C] Carbon tetrachloride/ White petrol

D] Turpentine oil

266] To check the dimensional accuracy of identical components, a dial test indicator is set-for t 6 Size and used as a comparator] What will you use to set to the dial test indicator?

A] Dial test indicator

B] Teeter gauge

C] Slip gauge

D] surface gauge

Dial test indicator Animation Videos

267] which one of the following statement about Sine bar is not correct?

A] Uses tow precision rollers kept on either side

B] Made of the Chromium steel

C] The surface is lapped

D] The centrelines of the holes will be inclined to the top surface

268] A slip gauge is a ----------

A] Rectangular block

B] Square block

C] Cubic block

D] Cylindrical block

269] In 4th SERIES of slip gauge, which one of the following range is correct in set 46 pieces

A] 1.0 to 9.0 mm.

B] 1.001 101.009 mm

C] 1.01 to 1.09 mm

D] 1.1'to_-1.9mm

270] In 5th SERIES of slip gauge, which one Of the following range is correct in set 46 pieces –

A] 100 to 100 mm '

B] 1.001 to 1.009 mm

C] 1.01 to 0.09mrn

D] 11 to 9mm

271] In 2NDS SERIES of slip gauge, which one of the following range IS correct in set of 45 pieces-

A] 1.0 to 9.0 mm

B] 1.001 to 1] 009 mm

C] 1.01 to 1.09 mm

D] 1.1 to 1.9mm

272] In 3RD SERIES of slip gauge, which one of the following range is correct in set 46 pieces –

A] 10.0 to 100 mm

B] 1.001 to 1.009 mm

C] 1.01 to 1.09 mm

D] 1.1 to 1.9 mm

273] In 1ST SERIES of slip gauge, which one of the following range is correct in set 46 pieces –

A] 0.001mm

B] 001mm

C] 0.1mm

D] 1.0mm

274] In 2ned SERIES of slip gauge, which one of the following STEP is correct in set of 46 pieces –

A] 0.001mm

B] 0.01 mm

C] 0.1 mm

D] 1-0 mm

275] In 3rd SERIES of slip gauge, which one of the following STEP Is correct in set 46 pieces

A] 0.001mm

B] 0.01mm

C] 0.1 mm

D] 1.0mm

276] A BSW threading tool is to be ground with an included angle of

A] 55◦

B] 60◦

C] 47.5◦

D] 29◦

277] The nose radius of a metric 'V' thread tool is

A] 0.144 x P

B] 0.25 x P

C] 0.414 x P

D] 0.0144 x P

278] While cutting metric external threads of coarse pitches, it is advisable to swivel the compound rest to

A] 45◦

B] 30◦

C] 60◦

D]90◦

279] The depth of B.I.S] metric thread is

A] 0.6403 x P

B] 0.6 x P

C] 0.6134 x P

D] 0.5 x P

280] Threading tools are checked for accuracy for the 60◦ angle by using a

A] Thread plug gauge

B] centre gauge

C] screw pitch gauge

D] tool angle gauge

Centre gauge Animation Videos

281] The number of threads per inch can be checked with a

A] tool gauge
B] metric rule by counting
C] ring gauge
D] screw pitch gauge
282] When threading, the carriage is moved along the ways by
A] a gear train on a track
B] the feed rod spline or key-way
C] the lead screw thred
D] the hand wheel
283] Thread chasers are used for
A] quick production of threads
B] maintaining an exact form of thread
C] cutting threads on hard materials
D] cutting threads on soft materials
284] Thread chasers are made out of
A] carbon steel
B] high speed steel
C] tool used
D] stainless steel
285] Chasers are used to cut
A] 'V' form threads only
B] square threads only
C] acme threads only
D] any form of threads
286] To cut M24 x 3 mm pitch internal threads, the core diameter of the job is
A] 27.00 mm
B] 24.50 mm
C] 21.00 mm
D] 24.00 mm
287] The depth of cut for M24 x 3 mm internal thread is
A] 0.5412 x 3
B] 0.6134 x 3
C] 0.5 x 3
D] 0.7 x 3
288] To cut 24 x 3 mm internal acme threads, the core diameter of the job is
A] 20.00 mm

B] 21.66 mm

C] 21.00 mm

D] 20.60 mm

289] The depth of cut for metric square threading is

A] 0.6 x P

B] 0.5 x P

C] 0.5412 x P

D] 0.6412 x P

290] To cut buttress thread, the depth of cut is

A] 0.5412 x P

B] 0.6 x P

C] 0.7 x P

D] 0.75 x P

291] For cutting acme threads, the tool is ground to an included angle of

A] 60°

B] 29°

C] 47.5°

D] 30°

292] The half-nut lever is used for

A] engaging the longitudinal feed on the carriage

B] taking up the slack in the cross-slide nut

C] changing from longitudinal to cross-feed

D] threads cutting

293] The bottom surface joining the two sides of adjacent thread (external thread] is...

A] Flank

B] Root

C] Crest

D] Pitch

294] The form of thread used in carpenters vice is...

A] Square

B] Acme thread

C] Sawtooth Thread

D] Knuckle thread

295] For transmitting very low torque.

A] Feather key

B] Gib head key

C] Woodruff key

D] Saddle key

296] Profile of key tends to weaken the shaft.

A] Feather key

B] Gib head key

C] Woodruff key

D] Saddle key

297] For transmitting unidirectional torque.

A] Feather key

B] Gib head key

C] Woodruff key

D] Saddle key

298] For transmitting heavy torque.

A] Feather key

B] Gib head key

C] Woodruff key

D] Saddle key

299] For transmitting very high torque of the impact type in both directions of rotation.

A] Gib head key

B] Woodruff key

C] Saddle key

D] Tangential key

300] Permits sliding or axial movement of the mat« ing piece on the shaft.

A] Feather key

B] Gib head key

C] Woodruff key

D] Saddle key

301] Can be withdrawn easily]

A] Feather key

B] Gib head key

C] Woodruff key

D] Saddle key

302] Preventive maintenance is ....]

A] The maintenance involves the use of sensitive instruments

B] The maintenance generally performed by operator himself

C] The work carried only when machine break down

D] plan to minimize the unforeseen break down

303] What is a break down maintenance?
A] Maintenance to minimize the unforeseen breakdown
B] Maintenance generally performed by operator himself
C] Maintenance involves replacement of worn out parts
D] Repairs work carried only when machine breakdown
304] The Routine Maintenance is ---------
A] it is planned maintenance to minimize the unforeseen breakdown
B] This type of maintenance involves the use of sensitive instrument
C] It is repair work carried only when machine breakdowns
D] This types of maintenance is generally performed by operator himself
305] Gear slip is due to
A] Worn out synchroniser
B] Worn out clutch disc
C] Dry main shaft bearing
D] Weak pressure spring of clutch.
306] If Less tension in belt
A] Belt slips.
B] Belt is damaged.
C] Belt whips.
D] Belt squeals.

307] If Misalignment in belt
A] Belt slips.
B] Belt is damaged.
C] Belt whips.
D] Belt squeals.

308] If Pulsating load on belt
A] Belt slips.
B] Belt is damaged.
C] Belt whips.
D] Belt squeals.
309] If High starting torque on pully
A] Belt slips.
B] Belt is damaged.
C] Belt whips.
D] Belt squeals.

310] If Shock load on belt

A] Belt slips.

B] Belt is damaged.

C] Belt whips.

D] Belt squeals.

311] If Centre distance between pulleys is more.

A] Belt slips.

B] Belt is damaged.

C] Belt whips.

D] Belt squeals.

312] This allows positive transmission of power at larger angles.

A] Slip type coupling

B] Plate coupling

C] Clamp coupling

D] Universal coupling

313] This disengages automatically when the. torque is higher than the friction generated by the spring and jaw.

A] Slip type coupling

B]] Plate coupling

C] Clamp coupling

D] Universal coupling

314] This can be used only when the shafts are in perfect alignment.

A] Slip type coupling

B] Plate coupling

C] Clamp coupling

D] Universal coupling

315] This does not permit any axial movement of the shafts.

A] Slip type coupling

B] Plate coupling

C] Clamp coupling

D] Universal coupling

316] This is used in automobile vehicles.

A] Slip type coupling

B] Plate coupling

C] Clamp coupling

D] Universal coupling

317] ------------ grooves are most commonly found on pulleys driven by V belts

A] 'V' Shaped

B] Slotted Shaped.

C] Square Shaped

D] Round Shaped

318] The hull gear wheel is driven

A] by a shaft

B] by a pinion

C] by sliding block.

D] None of above

319] Secures rope to small pipe or rim.

A] Slip knot

B] Bowline knot

C] Square knot

D] Sheep shank knot.

320] Pushes with drawl plate

A] Clutch cover

B] Release bearing

C] Release fingers

D] Clutch plate

321] Holds pressure plate with fly wheel

A] Clutch cover

B] Release bearing

C] Release fingers

D] Clutch plate

322] Used in gear box

A] Multi plate clutch

B] Dog clutch

C] Cone clutch

D] Diaphragm clutch

323] provides more frictional area

A] Multi plate clutch

B] Dog clutch

C] Cone clutch

D] Diaphragm clutch

324] smaller flywheel is used

A] Multi plate clutch

B] Dog clutch
C] Cone clutch
D] Diaphragm clutch
325] Spring acts as a release lever
A] Multi plate clutch
B] Dog clutch
C] Cone clutch
D] Diaphragm clutch
326] Type of drive mechanism
A] Pinion
B] Over running clutch
C] Plunger disk
D] Clutch
327] Prevents over speeding of pinion and armature
A] Pinion
B] Over running clutch
C] Plunger disk
D] Clutch
328] Accommodates wheel hub bearings.
A] Kingpin
B] Spring pad
C] Stub axle shaft portion
D] Track rod ball joints
329] Pushes with drawal plate
A] Clutch cover
B] Release bearing
C] Release fingers
D] Clutch plate
330] Takes thrust load
A] Crankshaft
B] Flywheels
C] Torque wrench
D] Thrust bearing
331]Distributor shaft is supported by
A] ball bearing
B] shell bearing
C] bush bearing
D] needle bearing

332] Extreme pressure additive (EPA] is mixed with cutting fluid for improving its power of.

A] Cooling

B] Lubrication

D] Production of the machined surface

C] Cleaning of cutting zone

333] The main purpose for using a lubricant in machine tools is to ------

A] Cool down the making parts

B] Prevent machine tool from heating

C] Wet the making parts for close contact

D] Minimize the friction between the making parts

334] The most important quality of any cutting fluid is

A] emulsification

B] specific heat

C] specific gravity

D] viscosity

335] By using coolants on workpieces we can choose

A] higher cutting speeds

B] lower cutting feeds

C] lower cutting speeds

D] heavy depth of cuts

336] Extreme pressure additive (EPA] is mixed with cutting fluid for improving its power of.

A] Cooling

B] Lubrication

C] Production of the machined surface

D] Cleaning of cutting zone

337] Filling up of the gap be» tween the bottom of the machine and the top of the floor or foundation block.

A] Wooden forms

B] Foundation bolts

C] Grouting

D] Template

338] Used to prevent any movement when the concrete is poured.

A] Wooden forms

B] Foundation bolts

C] Grouting

D] Template

339] Used to hold down the machine firmly on the foundation to prevent it from moving.

A] Wooden forms

B] Foundation bolts

C] Grouting

D] Template

340] Wooden patterns which represents the base of the machine and support bolts over the excavation.

A] Wooden forms

B] Foundation bolts

C] Grouting

D] Template

341] A voltage source produces an IR drop of 40V across a 20 ohms resistance, 60V across a 30 ohms resistance and 180V across a 90 ohms resistance all in series]How much is the applied voltage?

A] 180 V

B] 240 V

C] 100 V

D] 280 V

342] The initial function of a choke in a tube light circuit is to...

A] limit the starting current

B] induce high voltage

C] heat up the filament

D] limit the current after starting

343] The peak-to-peak voltage is 99V]how big is the effective value of the sine wave?

A] 70 V

B] 44.5V

C] 49.5 V

D] 35 V

344]A moving coil voltmeter reads 10 V AC]How big is the effective voltage?

A] higher

B] lower

C] the same

D]10% higher

345]A capacitor is connected across a 200 volt AC line, its minimum voltage rating should be...

A]100 volts

B] 200 Volts

C]300 volts

D]400 volts

346]How much is the nominal output voltage of a carbon zinc cell?

A]12V

B]1.5V

C]2.0V

D]2.2V

347]Cells are connected in series to..

A]increase the output voltage

B]decreases the output voltage

C]decrease the internal resistance

D]increase the current capacity

348] An unknown DC voltage is to be measured, which measuring range will you select first?

A]500V

B]50V

C]1.5 V

D]0.5V

349]Heat developed in a conductor is proportional to the...

A]square of the power

B]square of the resistance

C]square of the current

D]square of the time

350]The second function of a choke in a tube light circuit is to...

A]limit the starting current

B]induce high voltage

C]heat up the filament

D]limit the current after starting

351]A moving iron ammeter reads 10 A]how big is the peak current of the oscillation?

A]7.07 A

B]1.1414A

C]70.7 A

D]14.1 A

352]Power companies are interested in improving the power factor to

A]reduce line current

B]increase motor efficiency

C]increase volt-amperes

D]decrease power

353] In a RL parallel circuit, the opposition to total current is called...

A]reactance

B]resistance

C]a vector sum

D]impedance

354] An unknown direct current of micro ampere rating is to be measured, which measuring range will you select first?

A]20 micro amp

B]15 micro amp

C]150 micro amp

D]500 micro amp

355]The earth conductor provides a path to ground for..

A] leakage current

B] over current

C] high voltage

D] circuit current

356]Which appliance works on heating effect of electric current?

A]incandescent lamp

B]bimetallic thermostat

C]H R C fuse

D]toaster

357] connect two terminals of solenoid]

A] Pinion

B] Over running clutch

C] Plunger disk

D] Clutch

358] When the horn button is pressed the current flows to horn through

A] Horn switch

B] Solenoid coil

C] Battery

D] Chassis]

359] Turns core to magnet

A] Solenoid Switch

B] Actuating wire (when heated]

C] Ballast Resistors

D] Actuating wire (when cooled]

360]A capacitor increases the power factor value of an AC motor load when it is connected...

A] in series with the motor

B]in series with the starter

C]in parallel with the motor

D]in series with the main winding

361]Synchronous motor when used for power factor improvement should be...

A]under excited

B]over excited

C]loaded

D]running at no load

362]If a winding makes electrical contact with the metal case of the mixer motor the winding is...

A]grounded

B]open circuited

C]short circuited

D]loose connected

363]If the end shafts of a rotor turns blue it is an indication of...

A]scoring

B]overheating

C]freezing

D]burring

364] The depth of cut is given by

A] the top slide

B] the cross-slide

C] the compound slide

D] adjusting the tool

365] For mounting a lathe chuck

A] start it by hand and then turn the power on

B] mount it on by power

C] mount it by hand

D] mount it with the help of a hammer

366] The morse taper provided on drills used on lathe ranges between

A] MT1 to MT5

B] MT1 to MT4

C] MT0 to MT5

D] MT0 to MT4

367] Driving plates are used for

A] mounting fixtures and workpieces

B] driving shafts between Centre's with a lathe dog

C] facing operations only

D] internal operations only

368] Balancing is done in the face plate work

A] to increase the speed

B] to reduce the pressure on the tool

C] for uniform rotation of work

D] to get a good finish

369] A face plate is used to hold

A] a round job

B] a finished job

C] an irregular Job

D] a hollow job

370] Which is correct angle plate used with face plate

(A] Solid Type

(B] Box Type

(C] Adjustable Type

(D] None of them

371] Face plate is made from.....]

(A] Mild Steel

(B] Cast Iron

(C] Brass

(D] Aluminium

372] Which following accessories is use for odd an uneven job turning?

(A] Three Jaw Chuck

(B] Two Jaw Chuck

(C] Driving Plate

(D] Face Plate

373] An irregular shaped work piece is turned on a Lathe] Which one of the following work holding accessories is used?

A] Two Jaw chuck

B] Three Jaw chuck

C] Driving plate

D] Face plate

374] The pads of a steady rest are made of

A] carbon steel
B] lead
C] mild steel
D] brass
375] A steady rest is used
A] to hold jobs
B] for face plate work
C] to drive the job
D] to support the job

Lathe machine Animation Videos

376] A follower steady is held on the
A] lathe bed
B] lathe carriage
C] lathe spindle
D] tailstock
377] When turning long work pieces, the following is used
A sleeve
B change gear
C steady rest
D bracket]
378] Knurling operation is done at the
A] turning spindle speed
B] high spindle speed
C] 1/3 of the turning spindle speed
D] 1/2 of the turning spindle speed
379] Knurling is the operation of
A] shearing
B] forming
C] turning
D] pressing

INDUSTRIAL TRAINING INSTITUTE

Monthly Test-1, Marks- 20, Date:- _______________

(Every Question Carry Two Marks)

1-06] Benefit of SS system is ------

A] Increase in productivity

B] Increase in quality

C] Reduction in wastage of time

D] All of these

2-07] Safety is ----------

A] nobody's business

B] every bodise business

C] Some bodies business

D] The organization business

3-08] For basic categories of safety signs are available The meaning of"prohibition" sign ----

A] shows it must not be done

B] Shows what must be done

C] Warns the hazard or danger

D] Gives information of safety provision

4-09] Which one is a workshop safety?

A] Keep shop floor clean and free from grease, oil or other slippery materials

B] Stop the machine before changing the speed

C] Don't use cracked or chipped tools

D] Don't try to stop a running machine with hand

5-10] In Personal Protect Equipment (PPE] HELMET is used to

A] protect head

B] Protect eyes

C] Protect hands

D] Protect ears

6-11] Which of the following belongs to general safety?

A Have a worker in good attitude

B] The work clean and clear

C] Concentrate on your work

D] Keep the floor and gangways clean and clear

7-12] While grinding, which is used to protect the eyes?

A] Dark green glass

B] Mask

C] Sun glasses

D] Safety goggles

8-13] Which of the following is done for machine safety?

A] Check the oil level before starting the machine

B] Do things in a methodical way

C] Keep the floor and gangways clean and clear

D] Don't use dies and scarves

9-14] In Personal Protect Equipment (PPE], 'sleeves' is used to protect ---------

A] Face

B] Eyes

C] Ears

D] Hands

10-15] ABC stands for -------------

A] Automatic Breathing Control

B] Automatic Blood Control

C] Airway Breathing Circulation

D] Automatic Blood Circulation

INDUSTRIAL TRAINING INSTITUTE

Monthly Test-2, Marks- 20, Date:- ______________

(Every Question Carry Two Marks)

1-20] The size of the dividers are specified by the ---------

A] Total length of legs

B] Distance between the points when fully opened

C] Length of legs without points

D] distance between the pivot and the point

2-21] The instrument used to mark parallel lines, parallel to the datum edge is -

A] jenny caliper

B] Divider

C] Outside calliper

D] Inside calliper

3-22] Which one of the following is an indirect measuring tool?

A] Outside caliper

B] Vernier calliper

C] Steel rule

D] Outside micrometer

4-23] For cutting thin tubing, the most suitable pitch of the hacksaw blade is

A] 18mm

B] 14mm

C] 1mm

D] 08mm

5-24] For cutting solid brass, the most suitable pitch of the hacksaw blade is

A] 18mm

B] 14mm

C] 1mm

D] 08mm

6-25] A new hacksaw blade after a few strokes becomes loose because of the

A] Stretching of the blade

B] Wing-nut threads being worn out

C] Wrong pitch of the blade

D] Improper selection of the set of saws

7-26] While cutting small diameter pipes, it is advisable to watch regularly and ensure that

A] The cut is along the curved line

B] More saw teeth are in contract

C] The work is not overheated

D] Proper balancing of hacksaw is maintained

8-27] The vice clamps are used to

A] Protect hard jaws

B] Clamp the work pieces rigidly

C] Protect the finished surfaces

D] Prevent the movable jaw being filed

9-28] The reference surface during marking is provided by the

A] Surface gauge

B] Workpiece

C] Drawing of the work

D] Marking table surface

10-29] The size of an engineer's vice is specified by the

A] Length of the movable jaw

B] Width of the jaws

C] Height of the vice

D] Maximum opening of the jaws

INDUSTRIAL TRAINING INSTITUTE

Monthly Test-3, Marks- 20, Date:- ______________

(Every Question Carry Two Marks)

1-36] 'V' blocks are available in grades of

A] A & B

B] A,B & C

C] 1,2 & 3

D] 1 & 2

2-37] 'V' blocks of grade 'B' are made of

A] Cast iron

B] Mild steel

C] Steel

D] Cast steel

3-38] Ribs are given on the unmachined portion of the angle plate for

A] Easy handling

B] Convenience in manufacturing

C] Clamping while setting on machines

D] Rigidity and to prevent distortion

4-39] The slots on the angle plate are given for

A] Reducing weight

B] Aligning the work

C] Lifting using hooks

D] Accommodating bolts

5-40] The size of the angle plates is stated by

A] Weight

B] Length

C] Length x width

6-41] Name the punch used to locate the centre

A] Prick punch 30°

B] Prick punch 60°

C] Centre punch

D] Dot punch

7-42] The point angle of centre punch is --------

A] 30°

B] 50°

c] 900

D] 1200

8-43] Punches are used for forming ---------of any shape

A] Holes

B] Mining

C] Knurling

D] Reaming

9-44] Generally the length of the handle of the vice is ----------

A] 15 times the normal size of the vice

B] 25 times the normal size of the vice

C] 35 times the normal size of the vice

D] 45 times the normal size of the vice

45] Bench vice spindle is made of

A] mild steel

B] Cast iron

C] Tool steel

D] Bronze

INDUSTRIAL TRAINING INSTITUTE

Monthly Test-4, Marks- 20, Date:- _______________

(Every Question Carry Two Marks)

1-50] The point angle of scriber is -----------

A] 30°

B] 60°

C] 5° to 10°

D] 12° to 15°

2-51] The cutting angle for chipping cast iron is

A] 375?

B] 55?

C] 60?

D] 90?

3-52] The chisel will dig into the material when

A] The rake angle is more

B] The clearance angle is too low

C] The angle of inclination is more

D] The angle of inclination is too low

4-53] A slight convexity is given to the cutting edge to

A] Cut curved surfaces

B] Cut sharp corners

C] Prevent digging of the ends

D] Allow the lubricant to enter

5-54] Surface plates are made of

A] High grade cast steel

B] Fine-grained cast iron

C] Alloy steels

D] Wrought iron

6-55] The taper shank drills are held on the machine by means of

A] Chucks

B] Sleeves

C] Drift

D] Vice

7-56] Drill chucks are fitted on the drilling machine spindle by means of a

A] Knurled ring

B] Arbor

C] Drift

D] Pinion and key

8-57] The Morse taper provided on drills ranges between

A] MT 1 to MT 5

B] MT 1 to MT 4

C] MT 0 to MT 5

D] MT 0 to MT 4

9-58] A drift is used for

A] Drawing a drill location

B] Fixing chuck on the machine spindle

C] Removing a broken drill from the work

D] Removing the drill from the machine spindle

10-59] When the taper shank of the drill is larger than the machine spindle, the device to hold the drill is a

A] Drill sleeve

B] Taper socket

C] Drill drift

D] Chuck and key

INDUSTRIAL TRAINING INSTITUTE

Monthly Test-5, Marks- 20, Date:- ______________

(Every Question Carry Two Marks)

1-60] The suitable cutting fluid for drilling mild steel in a drilling machine is

A] Synthetic soluble oil

B] Neat oil

C] Distilled water

D] Soluble oil

2-66] In a remote place (no electricity available] a rail track is to be drilled Choose the right drilling machine

A] Radial drilling machine

B] Pillar drilling machine

C] Ratchet drilling machine

D] Sensitive drilling Machine

3-67] A drilling machine used by a carpenter for cabinet making is a

A] Ratchet drilling machine

B] Radial drilling machine

C] Breast drilling machine

D] Sensitive drilling machine

4-68] Which one of the following drilling machines is used for drilling holes where electricity is not available?

A] Bench drilling machine

B] Pillar drilling machine

C] Redial drilling machine

D] Ratchet drilling machine

5-69] Which one of the following drilling machine is used for heavy duty work?

A] Bench drilling machine

B] Pillar drilling machine

C] Radial drilling machine

D] Electric hand drilling machine

6-70] Drill chuck are held on the machine spindle by means of ------

A] arbor

B] Drift

C] draw-in bar

D] Chuck nut

7-71] Different speeds are obtained in a sensitive bench drilling machine by ----

A] Belt pulley mechanism

B] Hydraulic mechanism

C] Rack and Pinion mechanism

D] Cam and follower mechanism

8-72] Tap are re sharpened by grinding -----

A] Hutes

B] Threads

C] Diameter

D] Relief

9-73] The tapping drill size for M10 x 15 is ---------

A] 82

B] 83

C] 84

D] 85

10-74] A nut is to be made for a screw of M10XIS What should be the size of drilled hole?

A] 8-5 mm

B] 90 mm

C] 95 mm

D] 100 mm

INDUSTRIAL TRAINING INSTITUTE

Monthly Test-6, Marks- 20, Date:- ______________

(Every Question Carry Two Marks)

1-81] Which one of the following machine reamers is used to correct the misalignment between the reamer axis and the work axis?

A] Floating blade reamer

B] Machine jig reamer

C] Shell reamer

D] Chucking reamer

2-82] Accuracy or least count of a metric outside micrometer is ---------

A] 0-1 mm

B] 001 mm

C] 0001 mm

D] 002 mm

3-83] 1000 microns means -----

A] 1 mm

B] 1 m

C] 1000 mm

D] 10 cm

4-84] in a metric micrometer, a complete revolution of thimble advances -----------

A] 001 mm

B] 025 mm

C] 050 mm

D] 100mm

5-85] Ratchet Stop in the micrometer helps to ------------

A] Control the pressure

B] lock the spindle

C] Adjust the zero error

D] Hold the work piece

6-86] 1000 micron means ------------

A] 1 mm

B] 1 m

C] 1000 mm

D] 10 cm

7-87] What is the zero reading of a 50-75 mm outside micrometer?

A] 0000 mm

B] 001 mm

C] 2500 mm

D] 5000 mm

8-88] The value of the smallest division on sleeve of a metric outside micrometer is -----

A] 050 mm

B] 100 mm

C] 150 mm

D] 200 mm

9-89] Ratchet stop in the micrometer helps to ---------

A] control the pressure

B] Lock the spindle

C] Adjust the zero error

D] Hold the work piece

10-90] Least count of depth micrometer is

A] 0.5 mm

B] 0.2 mm

C] 0.001 mm

D] 0.01 mm

INDUSTRIAL TRAINING INSTITUTE
Monthly Test-7, Marks- 20, Date:- ______________
(Every Question Carry Two Marks)

1-96] The least count of a vernier bevel protractor is

A] 1"

B] 5'

C] 1?

D] 5 ?

2-97] The part of a vernier bevel protractor which is normally used as a reference base for measuring angles is the

A] Blade

B] Stock

C] Disc

C] Main scale

3-98] The part of a vernier bevel protector on which main scale divisions are marked is the

A] Stock

B] Dial

C] Disc

D] Adjustable blade

4-99] The part of a bevel protractor, which comes in contact with the inclined surface while measuring is the

A] Blade

B] Stock

C] Disc

D] Dial

5-100] The value of each division of the main scale of a vernier bevel protractor is

A] 5'

B] 1?

C] 5?

D]10?

6-101] The value of each division of the vernier scale of a bevel protractor is

A] 1?

B] 1?5'

C] 1?55'

D] 5'

7-102] The function of the Pedestal grinder includes -----

A] Sharpening of the cutting tool

B] Rough grinding

C] Both (a] & (b]

D] None of these

8-103] The type of abrasives used for the two wheels of Pedestal Grinder are-

A] Coarse and Coarse type

B] Fine and fine type

C] Coarse and fine

D] None of these

9-104] The Operation of shaping of the grinding wheel by dressers?

A] Dressing

B] Truing

C] Clogging

D] glazing

10-105] Dressing and truing of the grinding wheel are --------

A] Exactly the same operation

B] Clone with the same equment

C] Done only for coarse grinding wheel

D] Only for form grinding

INDUSTRIAL TRAINING INSTITUTE

Monthly Test-8, Marks- 20, Date:- ______________

(Every Question Carry Two Marks)

1-111] By using coolants on work pieces we can choose

A] Higher cutting speeds

B] lower cutting feeds

C] lower cutting speeds

D] heavy depth of cuts

2-112] Suitable for low cutting speed and feed rates

A] Carbon steel cutters

B] Sintered carbide tool cutters

C] Ceramics cutters

D] Diamond cutters

3-113] Extremely high cutting speed with low feed rate for precision finishing]

A] Carbon steel cutters

B] Sintered carbide tool cutters

C] Ceramics cutters

D] Diamond cutters

4-114] By using coolants on work pieces we can choose

A] higher cutting speeds

B] lower cutting feeds

C] lower cutting speeds

D] heavy depth of cuts

5-115] When using a diamond wheel for cutter grinding, a wheel speed of 1600/mm is recommended] What should be the depth of cut?

A] 0005-0025mm

B] 0025-004mm

C] 004-005mm

D] 005-005mm

6-116] The depth of cut for M24 x 3 mm internal thread is

A] 05412 x 3

B] 06134 x 3

C] 05 x 3

D] 07 x 3

7-117] The depth of cut for metric square threading is

A] 06 x P

B] 05 x P

C] 05412 x P

D] 06412 x P

8-118] To cut buttress thread, the depth of cut is

A] 05412 x P

B] 06 x P

C] 07 x P

D] 075 x P

9-119] Tennon slots are provided on arbor shoulder

A] To facilitate insertion of key between cutter and arbor at any position '

B] To facilitate positive power transmission to the arbor

C] To ' facilitate interchangeability of arbors and machines

D] To avoid loosening of arbor nut during cutting action]

10-120] In the BIS system of limits and fits, the grade of tolerance are represented by number Symbols and there are ---------i

A] 14 grades of tolerance

B] 16 grades of tolerance

C] 18 grades of tolerance '

D] 20 grades of tolerance

INDUSTRIAL TRAINING INSTITUTE

Monthly Test-9, Marks- 20, Date:- ______________

(Every Question Carry Two Marks)

1-126] Which one of the following is the clearance fit under the whole basic system?

A] 20 H7/p6'

B] 2067/211

C] ZOG/gll

D] 20H/g11

2-127] The three classes of fits as per BIS system aré

A] Clearance fit, interference fit and transition fit

B] Medium fit, push fit and tight fit

C] Flat fit, round fit and square fit

D] 'Sliding fit ', loose fit and shrinkage fit

3-128] Which one of the following tolerance specifications has a maximum dimensionless than 20 mm?

A] 20 +02,-03

B] 20 3202

C] 20 -02, 03 e

D]m 20 +500, ~03

4-129] Difference between the maximum and minimum limit is -------------------

A] Single informant

B] Basic shaft

C] Clearance

D] Tolerance

5-130] A shaft 55 running freely in bush bearing the type of fit is ---------

A] Clearance fit

B] Driving plate

C] shrinkage fit

D] None of the above

6-131] helps to tool to lifts up during return stroke

A] clapper box of shaper

B] rocker arm

C] pawl and ratchet

D] bull gear

7-132] pivoted at the bottom of the base

A] clapper box of shaper

B] rocker arm

C] pawl and ratchet

D] bull gear

8-133] meant for feed mechanism

A] clapper box of shaper

B] rocker arm

C] pawl and ratchet

D] bull gear

9-134] helps to tool to lifts up during return stroke

A] clapper box of shaper

B] rocker arm

C] pawl and ratchet

D] bull gear

10135] driven by pinion

A] clapper box of shaper

B] rocker arm

C] pawl and ratchet

D] bull gear

INDUSTRIAL TRAINING INSTITUTE
Monthly Test-10, Marks- 20, Date:- _______________
(Every Question Carry Two Marks)

1-141] During return stroke the clapper box is free to swivel about it.

A] Clapper box

B] Clapper block

C] Tool post

D] Hinged pen

2-142] Holds the tool or tool holder rigidly

A] Clapper box

B] Clapper block

C] Tool post

D] Hinged pen

3-143] Lifts during of return stroke

A] Clapper box

B] Clapper block

C] Tool post

D] Hinged pen

4-144] The movement of the vertical slide in achieved by stating this part.

D] Hinged pen

E] Swivel base

F] Vertical slide

G] Feed screw handle

5-145] Bench grinder are used for

A] Heavy duty work

B] Heavy and light duty work

C] Light duty work

D] Lather work

6-146] Bench Grinders are fitted on a

A] Base

B] Table]

C] Wheel guards

D] Conveyor

7-147] Which one of the following is the most commonly used Precision grinding machines?

A] Surface grinders

B] Tool cutter grinders

C] Cylindrical grinders

D] All of these

8-148] The feeler gauge is used for...

A] Checking surface roughness

B] Checking the redius of workpieces

C] Checking the gap between mating parts

D] Checking the accuracy of the hole locators

9- 149] Generally gauges are made out of

A] nickel chromium

B] mild steel

C] cast steel

D] H.S.S.

10-150] Generally gauges are used for

A] mass production

B] measuring the components

C] individual component

D] checking the dimensional accuracy

INDUSTRIAL TRAINING INSTITUTE

Monthly Test-11, Marks- 20, Date:- ______________

(Every Question Carry Two Marks)

1-156] Helical grooves and gears can be milled on this machine

A] Horizontal milling machine

B] Vertical milling machine

C] Universal milling machine]

D] Lathe machine

2-157] Slide movement on the column

A] Longitudinal feed

B] Cross feed

C] Vertical feed

D] Circular feed]

3-158] Slide movements on the knee

A] Longitudinal feed

B] Cross feed

C] Vertical feed

D] Circular feed]

4-159] Rotary table

A] Longitudinal feed

B] Cross feed

C] Vertical feed

D] Circular feed]

5-160] Table traverse]

A] Longitudinal feed

B] Cross feed

C] Vertical feed

D] Circular feed]

6-161] produces surface perpendicular to the axis of cutter

A] is face milling process

B] is side milling process

C] is plain milling process

D] is end milling process

7-162] producing surfaces vertical and flat, perpendicular to the machine arbor

A] is face milling process

B] is side milling process

C] is plain milling process

D] is end milling process

8-163] cutting is done at end and periphery to make slots

A] is face milling process

B] is side milling process

C] is plain milling process

D] is end milling process

9-164] The process done on plain milling machine

A] is face milling process

B] is side milling process

C] is plain milling process

D] is end milling process

10-165] The process done on vertical milling machine

A] is face milling process

B] is side milling process

C] is plain milling process

D] is end milling process

INDUSTRIAL TRAINING INSTITUTE

Monthly Test-12, Marks- 20, Date:- ______________

(Every Question Carry Two Marks)

1-171] More brittle in nature

A] Carbon steel cutters

B] Sintered carbide tool cutters

C] Ceramics cutters

D] Diamond cutters

2-172] is used to cut flutes on reamers

A] Equal double angle cutter

B] Bore type single angle cutter

C] Unequal double angle cutters

D] shank type single angle cutter]

3-173] is used to cut dovetail guide ways on a horizontal milling machine

A] Equal double angle cutter

B] Bore type single angle cutter

C] Unequal double angle cutters

D] shank type single angle cutter]

4-174] is used to cut 'V' grooves

A] Equal double angle cutter

B] Bore type single angle cutter

C] Unequal double angle cutters

D] shank type single angle cutter]

5-175] has two types as type 'A', type 'B' based on the diameter of the small end

A] Equal double angle cutter

B] Bore type single angle cutter

C] Unequal double angle cutters

D] shank type single angle cutter]

6-176] is Specified by mentioning two angles

A] Equal double angle cutter

B] Bore type single angle cutter

C] Unequal double angle cutters

D] shank type single angle cutter]

7-177] may or may not have cutting edges at flat side]

A] Equal double angle cutter

B] Bore type single angle cutter

C] Unequal double angle cutters

D] shank type single angle cutter]

8-178] Vertical milling attachment

A] face milling, boring, end drilling, 'T' slot milling

B] milling longer milling racks

C] mounted on the face of the column or the over arm

D] vertical milling attachment is provided

9-179] For using plain or universal milling machine as a vertical milling machine

A] face milling, boring, end drilling, 'T' slot milling

B] milling longer milling racks

C] mounted on the face of the column or the over arm

D] Vertical milling attachment is provided

10-180] Vertical attachments enable the horizontal milling machine to perform

A] face milling, boring, end drilling, 'T' slot milling

B] milling longer milling racks

C] mounted on the face of the column or the over arm

D] vertical milling attachment is provided

www.ingramcontent.com/pod-product-compliance
Ingram Content Group UK Ltd.
Pitfield, Milton Keynes, MK11 3LW, UK
UKHW021918190726
13853UKWH00002B/736

9 798886 847529